Mastering Online Marketing

Create business success through content marketing, lead generation, and marketing automation.

Learn email marketing, search engine optimization (SEO), and social media marketing with Facebook, Twitter, LinkedIn, and YouTube. Improve your Internet marketing results using web metrics and Google Analytics.

By Magnus Unemyr

Mastering Online Marketing

By Magnus Unemyr

6th September, 2015

Print ISBN-10: 1517057949
Print ISBN-13: 978-1517057947

Cover design: Bogdan Matei
Editing: Eric Anderson

All feedback welcomed:
feedback@unemyr.com

Limit of liability/disclaimer of warranty

Table of contents

Preface

I have developed websites since the beginning of Internet time in the middle of the 1990s. I have created them at work and for the businesses of friends and family. Later, the scope of my interest and work broadened into Internet marketing in a wider sense. I have been fortunate to use some of the most advanced Internet marketing tools available, and I will share what I have learned in this book.

For a long time, Internet marketing was primarily about having a website, and later about sending newsletter emails. When talking to business owners, managers, and others, it has become clear that to many, Internet marketing is still just about these two tools. Many business owners I have met from non-IT industries are proud to announce they have a great website, but fail to understand that this is no longer state-of-the-art, nor sufficient for success.

The Internet develops at warp speed, and modern online marketing is far from what it was only a couple of years ago. In fact, the majority of Internet marketing techniques of today are not about the website or monthly newsletter emails at all. The field has gone through a radical change in recent years, and so much more can be done to improve your performance and results.

I wrote this book to provide a concise, hands-on guide to how a business can use modern Internet techniques and tools to attract more visitors, convert more leads, and improve business results. The book provides an overview of Internet marketing of today, with practical advice and best-practice recommendations to improve your online success.

This is the book I wish I had when I was starting to learn about Internet marketing. I hope you will find it useful, and I would appreciate your feedback once you have read it. You can find my contact details at the end of the book. Also, please give an honest review on Amazon.

Before you start, I would like to mention that I am not associated with any of the companies mentioned in the book, and I own no stock in them. I get no benefits (financial or otherwise) from any of these companies. Products are mentioned because I have either used them and recommend them or because they are commonly used in the industry.

I hope you will enjoy reading this as much as I enjoyed writing it!

MAGNUS UNEMYR

www.unemyr.com

How this book is organized

Mastering Online Marketing provides a natural and stepwise progression of information, with a clear focus on practical and actionable knowledge that can be used right away.

The book is organized into these chapters:

- The **Introduction** provides the necessary background and an overview of Internet marketing as a foundation for later chapters. This chapter is about defining goals, inbound versus outbound marketing, the marketing funnel, customer journeys, buyer personas, leads segmentation, and more.

- **Attracting visitors** outlines the centerpiece of any Internet marketing effort: having a website and a blog to attract visitors. This chapter gives advice on how to use these tools as the basis for demand generation and further Internet marketing efforts.

- **The leads conversion process** explains how anonymous visitors are converted into identified leads, and outlines best practices for leads generation using call-to-action buttons, landing pages, registration forms, and thank you pages.

- **Content creation and digital assets** focus on how to create effective marketing assets that help build engagement with your audience. In this chapter, you will learn how to create documents and other offers that attract visitors and trigger them to convert to leads.

- **Email marketing** is about keeping and increasing the interest of your leads in an effective way until they are ready to make the purchase. This chapter is about mailshots and drip email campaigns, but also covers legal and technical matters related to successfully sending marketing emails.

- **Search engines, ads, and more** provides information on search engine optimization (SEO), search engine marketing, search keyword analysis, and various types of advertisement options, including display advertisement and retargeting.

- **Social media and content sharing platforms** explains how social media and content publishing platforms can be used in the online marketing mix. This chapter covers how you can use popular channels like Facebook, LinkedIn, Twitter, YouTube, and SlideShare to attract and engage leads.

- **Marketing automation systems** outlines a new type of integrated tools that completely change the game in Internet marketing. This chapter explains how these systems can be used for visitor tracking and lead profiling, automatic leads generation and nurturing, content personalization, automated workflows, and more.

- **Optimizing results with A/B testing** explains how you can test and improve the effectiveness of various marketing components by comparing the results of alternative implementations. It covers how A/B testing can be done for emails, calls-to-action, landing pages, and more.

- **Web analytics 1 – Measure and improve** presents web analytics and shows how it can be used to understand how your website performs, and how it can be improved. This chapter introduces Google Analytics and shows how this free tool provides unprecedented insight into how your website is used.

- **Web analytics 2 – Monitor results** explains how to measure your business success and track campaign results. It also shows how Google Analytics can be used to track goals, understand funnel performance, and analyze online and offline campaigns.

- **Web analytics 3 – Advanced concepts** covers how you can integrate other online and offline data sources, and explains how web metrics can be used for other types of advanced analysis. This chapter shows how to understand search keyword effectiveness and use event tracking and intelligence alerts in Google Analytics.

- **Other Internet marketing tools** highlights additional software tools to use in your marketing work. This chapter outlines useful tools for running virtual meetings and seminars, publishing customer surveys, and providing self-running interactive presentations and demos.

- **The future of Internet marketing** contains a prediction on how Internet marketing will progress in the coming years. In my mind, predictive marketing automation systems, adaptive content, web analytics, big data, and the Internet of Things (IoT) will drive Internet marketing to new heights.

- **Final thoughts** includes my closing remarks on the incredible possibilities now available to marketers, and the growing privacy concerns that emerge when increasing amounts of personal data is gathered and cross-referenced.

- **Appendix 1 – Internet networking basics** outlines what you need to know about how the Internet works. It explains key technical concepts like IP-addresses and ports, domain names and subdomains, and what a URL is.

- **Appendix 2 – Website basics** explains the most important concepts in website implementation and hosting, including web servers and content management systems, as well as key technologies like HTML, CSS, JavaScript, and cookies.

Introduction

Internet marketing is developing at a breathtaking speed, and keeping up with all the developments is almost impossible. Unless you work with it as a full-time career, you are unlikely to have a complete picture of where the field stands today. Even then, you may not be aware of what an integrated marketing automation system or a video marketing platform can do.

This situation can be frustrating to business owners and others who need to use Internet marketing in their work, but do not have the time to keep up with the technical evolution. Among a thousand other tasks, you also need to know the whats, hows, and whys to make your online presence a business success.

What was tried and true not long ago has been replaced with new strategies and truths, and long gone are the days when online marketing only meant having a website and sending monthly newsletter emails. There are so many more components involved today.

Many books already exist on Internet marketing. Is there a need for another one? I would argue yes. Of all the books I've read on this over the years, none of them offered what I'm looking for: the *one* book that provides the grand overview of it all, including the latest state-of-the-art concepts with enough detail to give practical and actionable knowledge that can be useful immediately.

This book does not take an academic approach, but tries to provide hands-on advice of real value to practitioners who want to get started with Internet marketing, or take the next step to improve current efforts. With this guide, you should be able to pick up and use these new skills immediately.

So let's jump in. What is the first step to building your online marketing presence?

To start, the objective of a website should be clear, with measurable goals to signal success. Without an understanding of what drives your success, you cannot measure the effectiveness of your website and other marketing efforts. To do this. you should setup and continuously monitor the most important goals using Key Performance Indicators (KPIs). Don't worry, I will explain this later.

It is also important to be conscious of the radical change currently happening in modern Internet marketing. Outbound mass marketing techniques that interrupt and annoy the recipients are being replaced with inbound and personalized content marketing that aim to give the targeted audience more of what they already want. This paradigm shift serves potential customers with valuable and useful knowledge at the right time, creating a positive buyer experience. It is not about pushing your sales pitch anymore, but rather serving potential customers with trust-building and educational content that helps them choose you over your competition.

Concepts like buyer persona definitions, the marketing funnel, customer journey paths, and leads segmentation are important to understand. Likewise, strategies for attracting more visitors and knowing how to convert them into leads are vital for success. While this book covers traditional techniques like having a website and sending newsletter emails, more focus is put on generating organic traffic using a blog, and efficient lead generation strategies.

New leads aren't usually ready to buy right away, so you will have to deploy various leads nurturing strategies to help them along the customer journey towards the purchase decision. Today, refined leads nurturing strategies can help improve the engagement with your leads until they make a purchase decision. This book will tell you how.

In the new era of inbound marketing, content creation is king. You need to know how to create effective digital marketing assets like white papers, eBooks, videos, infographics, and case studies. Your digital assets should help generate traffic by attracting new visitors, converting them into leads, and supporting leads nurturing. There are best practices in developing different types of digital marketing assets, and we'll cover this in detail in the chapter on content creation.

Social media and video marketing channels are increasingly becoming a viable option in Internet marketing too, particularly on Facebook, LinkedIn, Twitter, and YouTube. You can use these channels in conjunction with other online marketing efforts to set up a marketing system where different parts interact and support each other.

In modern Internet marketing, there are many independent tools and techniques that work together towards the goal of attracting more visitors, converting them to leads, and finally into customers. Unfortunately, using separate tools is not always the best strategy. For this reason, fully integrated marketing automation systems are becoming increasingly popular, and the chapter on marketing automation will explain what these tools can do in quite some detail.

Unless you have studied high-end marketing automation systems already, I can guarantee you will be amazed to learn what is possible these days. Most website owners (not to mention the general public) are unaware of what advanced capabilities are now available using leading-edge tools. Companies already using these systems want to keep this to themselves to preserve the advantage over their competitors. But soon, you too will know the secret and understand the power of these systems.

Finally, you cannot measure success and improve upon it without careful monitoring. This can be done using web analytics tools, which provide statistics and metrics on website usage. This metering is the feedback loop of the goals and KPIs you should have defined early in your online marketing efforts.

In fact, web analytics is a lot more than measuring your top-level business performance. Several chapters are dedicated to recording and analyzing the behavior of your visitors and the effectiveness of your online presence. This book explains how to do this using Google Analytics, a free and powerful web tool available to anyone.

If you are completely new to Internet technology, you may want to read Appendix 1 on Internet networking basics and Appendix 2 on website basics before jumping in. There I provide the necessary technical foundation for understanding the other chapters. For example, if you do not know the difference between a web server and a content management system, or what a URL or cookie is, you should read the appendices first.

In practice, small businesses may not have the time or resources to start using all of the concepts presented in this book, at least not initially. But quickly getting an overview of the options and best practices is key to successful results. You can always expand your campaigns and improve over time.

I often refer to selling a product or service as the final goal, as this is the aim for most businesses. If you are representing a non-profit organization or some other type of website, your goal may be different. For example, it can be getting more blog subscribers, more members to a golf club, raise more funds for medical aid, or any other goal that fits your organization. In such case, just replace the final goal of getting more customers with your own objective.

The following section provides a short overview of the major concepts in Internet marketing before we dive into more details. This is a top-level view of how it all fits together, and serves as a background for the rest of the book. Later chapters will discuss these topics in more detail and provide practical, hands-on advice in specific areas.

Setting goals and KPIs

Before spending time and money on Internet marketing, you should be entirely clear on what your objectives are. This may be obvious, but how to set this up may not be.

For example, do you want to generate more leads, or get more sales transactions in the web shop? Perhaps you're trying to reduce the number of support questions to your service team, or spread the word about your charity's work overseas? Consider carefully what your primary aim is, and optimize different parts of your website and online marketing efforts accordingly.

Once the main objective is clear, you need to define what measurable goals you have. A goal is a user-initiated action that signals to you that a visitor has taken another defined step towards buying a product, or done something else of direct or indirect value to your business.

In web metrics, a goal is not a vague measure like the number of visitors or pageviews you hope to get, but rather it should be something that has an apparent relation to reaching the objective of selling a product. Goals are specific events that affect your business success, either directly or indirectly.

In addition to sales transactions, there are other goals worth monitoring. These include the number of requests for quotes, requests for free product samples, the number of software downloads, or something else that a potential customer usually does before buying your product. But a goal can also be other types of goals that signal success, such as reducing the number of submitted support questions.

Dependent on your business, you may end up with many goals you want to monitor. In fact, it may become difficult to get an at-a-glance top-level overview of your current business health if you have more than five goals to track. To solve this, you will have to define Key Performance Indicators (KPIs). These are a limited set of goals that measure your business success at an overview level.

You will monitor the KPIs more regularly than other goals to track the performance and gain insight into the current status of your business. The KPIs will tell you if your website results are going up or down, and provide a measure to gauge trends and comparative data over time. You should only pick the most important goals as KPIs, or you will not see the forest through the trees.

With the KPIs defined, continuously monitoring the result can provide valuable insights. For example, if your average purchase cycle is two months, you can expect a sales drop eight weeks from now if the number of requests for quotes decreases this month. The same may be signaled if you get fewer downloads of the evaluation version of your software product or requests for free product samples.

In effect, KPIs help monitor the health of your business at measurable key points in your online marketing system.

The radical change in online marketing

Internet marketing is in a state of transition. Traditional marketing approaches push the same information to everyone, hoping someone cares enough to read it. This is usually not the case. To make matters worse, the message may interrupt the recipient at inappropriate times and cause animosity to the company.

This is called outbound marketing and typically includes having to pay for advertisements or sending emails to thousands of addresses you have bought. In the end, you spend a lot of money and effort distributing information the receiver does not want to read.

For paid advertisements, your marketing reach is in direct relation to the size of your marketing budget. When the money is spent and the advert has expired, the investment will not give you any further results. Luckily, this is no longer the best recipe for success.

While this strategy may still work, Internet marketers have increasingly started to invert the process and provide content that the intended audience *wants* to read. Therefore, *they come to you* when the *time is right* for *them*. This is called inbound marketing, or content marketing.

By offering valuable or educational content such as blog articles, eBooks, white papers, and training videos, people interested in products like yours will find you using Internet search engines. They can then start to interact with you and your offerings when they are ready to receive more information.

Because visitors are actively looking for information from you, inbound marketing is more engaging and captures the lead when they are most interested in what you have to offer. We'll cover traditional marketing approaches, but the majority of this book will cover these new and effective techniques.

The good news is that inbound marketing will increase your sales at a reduced advertisement budget, if done properly. The downside is that you will have to create a lot of digital marketing content instead. However, once content is created and published online, it will continue to generate visitors and leads for years to come with no further work or investment. The marketing value does not stop when the ad budget expires.

The marketing funnel

The marketing funnel is the set of phases a potential customer passes through in the process of going from being a stranger to your company to becoming persuaded and making a purchase decision. It is the marketer's view of how potential customers pass through the buying process.

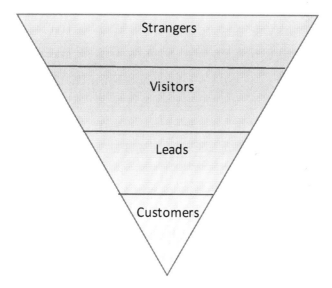

The marketing funnel contains these steps:

- Initially strangers are attracted to come to your website using means like search engines (such as Google), social media, paid advertisements, or offline marketing.

- When strangers arrive at your website, they become anonymous visitors.
- If visitors register their contact information in a form on the website, they become leads.
- Once a lead has been persuaded to give you the purchase order, you close the deal and they become a customer.

The top of the marketing funnel is wide because many strangers come to your website, thus becoming visitors. The middle of the funnel is narrower since not all visitors will register their contact information and become a lead. The bottom is smaller still, since many leads don't buy anything.

Sometimes a fifth step is added to the marketing funnel when delighted customers become promoters and start to spread the word about your fantastic product to new strangers, and the process starts all over again.

Each potential customer is in one of the stages in the marketing funnel at a given time, and the strategies to move him or her forward towards the purchase decision is different along the way. The types of marketing information to offer the customer are also different at various stages in the funnel.

To get more sales, you need to optimize your efforts for each phase of the marketing funnel to:

- Attract more strangers
- Convert more anonymous visitors into identified leads
- Convince more leads to buying your product

This book will teach you up-to-date techniques for improving all these areas.

The customer journey

The marketing funnel is your view of how a potential customer passes through the buying process, and the customer's journey is the same process seen from the other side.

Customer's go through an information gathering process with specific touch points on their way to making the purchase decision.

With more information about what actions leads typically take before making a purchase decision, and where a particular visitor is in that process, you can offer targeted marketing information at the right time.

- In the awareness stage, potential customers realize they have a problem they might want or need to have solved. This is early in the customer journey and your marketing information should be focused on problem solving or improvement topics.
- In the consideration stage, potential customers make an effort to learn more to find a solution to their problem. This is in the middle of the customer journey when they are searching for more solution-oriented and detailed knowledge of your product's capabilities.
- The end is the decision stage, where the potential customer wants to know how your product compares or performs compared to another vendor's products. Here you can focus on product information or comparisons, and relationship building using for example webinars, consultations, or product demos.

For each of these stages, the potential customer may have several or many touch points with you, and you should offer marketing content to support that. In fact, you can even chart the customer journey and plan the unique content you want to provide to potential customers at each stage of the customer journey. This is called the customer journey map.

Buyer personas

Before you start any active marketing, you should also consider who you want to market and sell to. With a clear picture of your target market, you will be more successful and see better results. Buyer personas define who you want to reach, what type of marketing information will be most successful with them, and the type of websites they frequent.

What is a buyer persona? This is an ideal fictional customer that helps you understand who you market to. A buyer persona is not a real person, it is a generalization of clients with similar behaviors, needs, or wishes, and perhaps demographic information.

You probably have several different buyer personas in your business. For example, a company selling boats and boating equipment may identify these as the most significant buyer personas:

- Joe the young professional looks for a speedboat. He is interested in fast and cool boats and plans to use it to bring friends out for fun weekends. He is likely to be 20-30 years old and have a decent salary and few worries in life.

- Mark the father wants to bring his wife and small children out for short trips during good conditions and worries more about safety and comfort than speed and style. He is probably between 35-50 years of age and needs to use most of his income on other things.

- Caroline the teenager loves windsurfing, and is entirely focused on the sports experience. While she does not have a good income yet, she prefers windsurfing gear from well-known vendors with a high coolness factor.

With a clear picture of what buyer personas you want to reach, you can adapt your website and other online marketing content to fit them perfectly. In short, you should care less about having any stranger coming to your website, and focus instead on attracting the right visitors who best match your product—and are most likely to buy it.

By identifying personas, you define the categories of the people you want to reach. All your marketing content thereafter should be optimized to fit your buyer personas. Clearly defined buyer personas also help you discover where your prospective customers spend time on the Internet, which tells you where to promote your business. Start to promote to your most important buyer persona first, and over time you can add campaigns and content better optimized for the other ones.

Well-defined buyer personas can give better value for money in promotion investments if your marketing content is consistently optimized for them.

Segmentation

Segmentation is about filtering your leads database in different ways, with the purpose of providing focused marketing information to your leads. With a segmented address list, you can send a campaign mailshot to only those leads that are most likely to be interested in that offer. A discount offer on women's clothing may not be as effective if you send it to men, for example.

Segmentation provides you with the means to send certain marketing messages to special groups of leads in your database. Segmentation can be done based on who the leads are (their demographics) or what they have done (their past behavior).

- With demographic filtering, you segment leads based on where they live, their sex, age, or income. Other types of information may be placed in this category as well, such as job title, company size, industry, and interests.

- With behavior filtering, you segment leads based on what they have done previously, for example what emails they have opened and clicked, what social media interactions they have had with your company, what web pages or blog articles have they read, or how often they return to your website.

Always try to provide a relevant marketing message by segmenting your leads, and only send marketing information to groups of leads that have an interest in that topic.

Attracting visitors

To reduce your marketing spending, you will need to find free or inexpensive ways to attract visitors to your website. The trick here is digital content and search engines.

Google and other search engines index websites and recommend them when someone searches for a particular set of keywords that match the contents of a web page. By ensuring your pages turn up early in the search engine result pages, it is likely the person searching for the keywords will click the links to visit your site.

The more web pages you have with information related to a specific set of search keywords, the greater the chance one or more of those pages ends up early in the search results and gets clicked. In short, by writing several web pages touching on relevant subjects, more visitors can be sent to you from search engines such as Google, Bing, or Yahoo.

How do you write a lot of web pages with information related to the same search keywords? One strategy is to have a large website with lots of pages containing similar information targeting the same keywords. This only works to a certain extent, as the website eventually starts to look weird if you have too many pages with similar or unnatural content.

The better approach, now being used by many online marketers, is to complement the website with a blog. Since a blog is essentially a flow of informal articles on almost any topic, it is much easier to create one with many articles. They can all touch upon similar—or for that matter, different—subjects. It looks natural to have many blog articles covering similar topics, as long as you modify them somewhat and mix them with other topics in between.

With inbound marketing, having a lot of content is everything. Create a large website with many web pages, but most importantly, create an active blog that over time will contain hundreds of articles discussing things at least partially related to your product or industry.

The process is similar to fishing with a net: if you throw out a small net into the lake, you will only get a couple of fish. But with a net ten times larger, you will get ten times more fish. The same is true for online content. The more web pages and blog articles you have on a subject, the bigger the chance search engines will send traffic (visitors) to you whenever someone searches for relevant keywords.

Receiving visitors from search engines (this is called organic traffic) is one thing, but you also want to delight and impress them to keep them around for as long as possible. This allows you to engage with them more, expose them to your thought leadership, and present trust building content.

Your digital content should always be of high quality, with information that is genuinely useful or valuable to your visitors. If visitors only get a sales pitch, they are unlikely to hang around your site. To keep their attention, offer information, training material, or thoughts that are of genuine interest, have educational value, or otherwise solve a problem or pain point for them.

Converting visitors to leads

Provided you have a website and blog to attract visitors with the help of search engines, how do you turn these anonymous visitors into leads you know something about (in particular, their contact information)? The primary means of converting anonymous visitors into identified leads is to make them fill out their contact information in a registration form.

To give their contact information to you, they must trust you and be delighted with the valuable information or knowledge they have gained by visiting your website or blog. But this is often not enough, since many people won't submit their information just because they like your site or have been asked to.

You will have to provide something of real value in return for their contact details. In short, the trick is to offer a digital asset they desire. This can be something like a white paper, a video tutorial, an eBook, a checklist, an Excel calculation formula, a Word document template, or a training webinar. To get access to the digital asset, visitors have to register their contact information in a web form.

In effect, visitors buy the digital asset and pay with their contact information. Once you have the details of a lead, you can start to engage with him or her, and set up various nurturing strategies to move the lead further down the customer journey and closer to the sale.

Leads nurturing

Your marketing efforts attracted new visitors to your website and converted them into leads using registration forms. Now your goal is likely to make a new lead buy something from you, but he or she may not be ready for a purchase decision just yet.

Your job is to nurture the lead until the time is right, making sure your company or product continues to be in the top of his or her mind. At the same time, you should try to make the leads engage more deeply with you over time. This leads nurturing is usually done by sending automatic emails.

Not too many years ago, online leads nurturing was almost only about sending the same batch email to everyone in a database, often in the form of a monthly newsletter email. While sending newsletter emails are becoming less effective, email marketing is not dead and is not likely to go away for a long time. But to be effective, your emails need to be more personalized and relevant to your recipients.

Today, online leads nurturing includes sending a series of emails with a consistent purpose when the lead engages with you in some way. Using a well-designed leads nurturing concept increases the likelihood you are remembered when the time is right, and that your product or service is shown in the best light.

Measuring success

To measure if you are successful with your online presence, you need to know how well you perform on the most important metrics. It is essential to record and analyze the origin and behavior of website visitors, the conversion ratio of various marketing campaigns, and the effectiveness of other related online and offline marketing efforts.

This is done using web analytics tools, which help you understand where your visitors come from, what web pages attract or scare them away, how they move around your site, how different segments of visitors behave in relation to others, and to what extent goals are fulfilled.

By measuring and analyzing your current situation, and how changes affect the results, you can improve the user experience and increase your goal conversion ratio. Measuring, analyzing, modifying, and testing the results is a continuous process that should be performed frequently. It is not a one-time activity.

Measuring success using web analytics tools ties back to the goals and KPIs you should have defined for your online presence.

Chapter summary

In this chapter, we discussed the importance of setting goals, and how interruptive and annoying outbound mass marketing strategies are increasingly being replaced with inbound content techniques. This provides educational and useful information that the potential customer actively looks for and finds valuable, thus helping them to come to you and chose your product.

The marketing funnel and the customer journey was described, as were buyer personas and leads segmentation. These are key to understanding what marketing content is suitable for whom, and when. We also looked at a quick overview of attracting visitors using a website and blog, along with information on how to convert anonymous visitors into identified leads.

Leads nurturing using different email marketing strategies were covered, as well as an introduction to website usage analysis with web metrics and Google Analytics.

The next chapter provides information on how to attract visitors.

Attracting visitors

Up until a few years ago, attracting new visitors organically was done by having search engines like Google index your web pages and hoping they send traffic to your website. To improve the results, search engine optimization techniques were often used. This has not changed, but the concept is now extended by also having a blog that adds to the amount of traffic search engines send to you.

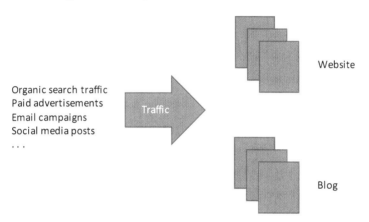

The website, and increasingly the blog, are your prime mechanisms for attracting new visitors. In addition to getting organic traffic, the website or the blog are usually the destination of various marketing campaigns, such as paid adverts, social media channels, or offline marketing. They should therefore be the centerpiece of any online marketing strategy.

The Website

Your website should, of course, look fabulous, with a consistent coloring and typeface scheme, beautiful layout and graphics, and modern and intuitive navigation controls, slideshows, and other widgets. Furthermore, the website needs to be responsive and auto-adapt its layout when visitors browse the Internet using mobile devices with a small screen. It should also contain a lot of engaging and useful information on your products and services.

In fact, the more web pages with lots of text information, the better. This is because search engines like Google can only drive traffic to your website if your pages contain the information Internet visitors are searching for. A website with mostly stunning photos (perhaps with text painted into the bitmap image) are entirely ineffective from a search engine optimization point of view. Don't forget: search engines can only look in text. Include relevant text on your website if you want search engines to send visitors your way. Lots of it.

Designing a great website is a huge subject of its own, and I leave this for other books to cover. For example, check out *HTML and CSS: Design and Build Websites* by Jon Duckett, *Learning Web Design: A Beginner's Guide to HTML, CSS, JavaScript and Web Graphics* by Jennifer Niederst Robbins, or *Don't Make Me Think* by Steve Krug. Or search for "website design" in your favorite bookshop. There will be no shortage of other books covering the subject. Additional information on a more technical level is also presented in Appendix 2 – Website basics.

We cover a lot of topics outside of websites in this book, but having an effective online presence starts there. Without a website, you can't make use of the other online marketing tools either. Make sure your website looks great and contains all the information needed for both your visitors and search engines to be happy.

The Blog

Apart from the regular company website, the blog is the other major tool you can use to attract visitors. Some years ago, blogging was mostly confined to teenagers writing about their personal life, but things have changed and having a blog is now a critical asset in the Internet marketing strategy of any company.

The key to this is that the website outlining your product offering will typically have a finite set of web pages, and they have to be written in corporate marketing language to make the website look professional. As such, it may be difficult to add a large number of additional web pages in a way that feels natural to website visitors. In particular, it becomes difficult to add pages with slightly more informal content and language that may be needed to engage with your audience on a personal level.

Since being found by search engines is crucial to getting more potential customers to see you, having more pages published increases your chances of search engines sending traffic your way. A blog is a perfect vehicle for this.

There is absolutely nothing wrong with your existing leads and customers visiting your blog frequently; in fact, it is great and can have many positive effects, including leads nurturing, thought leadership, and brand building. But one of the primary purposes of the blog is to fill it with many (perhaps hundreds of) blog articles over time. Use the blog to add as many pages as possible on the Internet, thus increasing the chances Google searches result in traffic to your site.

The great thing with blog articles is they stay "forever" on the Internet. It requires some effort to write a blog article, but once it is published, it will remain on the Internet for years, continuing to attract traffic from search engines like Google with no additional effort or expense on your part. The marketing value does not stop when the advertising budget is exhausted.

Blog hosting

A blog is often hosted on a different server from your regular website (but it doesn't have to be). If so, hyperlinks on your website promoting the blog may open it in a different browser window. There are many independent blog hosting solutions available on the Internet, and you can integrate it into your standard website if you prefer.

If your blog is not hosted on your company website, I recommend using a subdomain like blog.mycompany.com if your site is on www.mycompany.com. This means your blog uses your domain name (mycompany.com), which ensures that any blog traffic helps improve the search engine authority of your regular website and vice versa. I write more on website authority in a later chapter, but for now consider it a score of how important search engines think your website is.

In particular, you want to ensure that your blog does not use the domain name of the blog platform supplier, such as mycompany.somebloghosting.com, as your traffic will help improve their search engine authority instead of yours.

Blog article title and content

The blog should cover topics from your industry or pain points of your readers, and not promote or sell your products or company other than as a side effect. I try to follow these rules when writing blog articles:

- A catchy title containing the search keywords I want to get traffic from
- Minimum 750-1000 words of text
- The text must contain the targeted search keywords a couple of times, but not so often to make the writing feel forced or awkward. A few times is enough.
- Minimum one photo or graphic to spice up the article
- A personal, warm, and friendly writing style
- Genuinely helpful, informative, and educational content, without strong product promotion. Alternatively, share your thoughts on something that relates to your industry

The first point is important. A great title is everything, both for search engines and human readers. It is commonly said that you should spend half the time writing the blog article, and the other half coming up with a great title. Make sure the title contains the search keywords you want to optimize the blog post for and make it attractive for human readers too. For some reasons, numbered lists seem to generate more clicks, as do words in square brackets.

Examples of this are:

- 7 best ways to travel Europe
- Become a gardener in 15 steps
- Learn more about slow cooking [eBook]
- Interview with Tim Cook [of Apple fame]

Since a blogger is supposed to write many blog articles frequently, it is easy to run out of ideas for new blog posts. In fact, the problem is large enough for people to create blog topic or title generators that auto-generate ideas for blog articles. Search for "blog title generator" to find a few of them.

For search engines to find your article using the search phrase "backpacking Vietnam", these keywords need to be present in the title, as well as a couple of times in the article copy. However, be sure not to add the keywords too many times (known as keyword stuffing) as this may cause search engines to reduce your ranking as a penalty. More on this in the section on search engine optimization.

In fact, you should probably write several different blog articles targeting the same search keywords to have more articles fishing for traffic from that specific search phrase. Having a number of articles targeting the same keywords increases the likelihood at least one will catch some of the traffic. Just make sure to modify the title and copy (body text) enough to make it look like a different post, even if they cover almost the same topic (but perhaps from a different angle). Post them a few weeks apart so as not to bore your frequent readers, who will otherwise notice the repetition.

I have also found it useful to write blog articles that ask questions that don't need to be answered in the blog article, like "Is Porsche better than Ferrari?" In the article, just outline some pros and cons, and let the reader judge. There's no need for you to provide an answer to the question, it is simply an excuse to publish an additional blog article for Google and other search engines to find.

Another idea is to ask industry influencers if you can email some interview questions to them, and publish their answers in a blog article. If you are selling outdoor sports equipment, a nice blog article could be, for example, "What the mayor of [YOUR CITY] thinks about the new mountain trails."

Have you recently created some new digital assets or other offers that can be promoted? Be sure to write blog articles like:

- Learn more on Molecular Gastronomy [new training video]
- Read our new eBook on digital photography
- Visit us at the [EVENT NAME] Expo in New York next week

Your blog articles should provide links back to your website, or to other blog articles containing relevant information. This provides more visibility for your other pages and offers, and lets the reader engage more deeply with you for a longer time.

Remember the buyer personas we talked about earlier? Make sure each of your blog posts is targeted at a particular buyer persona, such as "Joe the development manager" or "Carol the software developer". They have different interests, problems, and pain points, and may like different writing styles as well. Ensure that when you write each blog article, you adapt it for a particular buyer persona to make it a perfect fit for that person.

Write blog posts with different targets, if you need to. The more, the better.

Blog frequency

How often do you need to write new blog posts? I'd say at least once a week, more often if you can. However, when you start the blog, you will need to fill it with ten or so articles immediately, before too many visitors start coming. Otherwise they may deem it useless and not come back.

The more blog posts you have, the greater the chance potential readers will find an article using search engines. In all cases, make sure the articles are genuinely helpful to the visitors, providing high-quality reading, without too much apparent product promotion.

Chapter summary

This chapter outlined how to attract visitors using a website and a blog, including details on how to set up the blog and write effective blog articles. While many Internet marketing strategies involve things outside of the website, it is still the centerpiece of it all, with the blog as the second most important part.

The next chapter looks at how to convert anonymous visitors into identified leads.

The leads conversion process

Having many anonymous website visitors is great, but you must convert them into leads if you want to do any active marketing to them. There is a well-defined process for turning anonymous website visitors into identified leads. This is where the rubber hits the road—you need to get this right to get performance out of your online marketing.

So you have a new anonymous visitor to the website. How do you get his or her contact information? By asking for it, of course! The problem is, contact information is not easily shared these days. You have to offer something of value in return.

This is where digital assets, call-to-action buttons, landing pages, registration forms, and thank you pages all come into play. If this sounds like Swahili to you, don't worry. It isn't all that complicated, and they all interact to set up a working leads generation system.

- Digital assets are something valuable visitors want to get
- Call-to-action (CTA) buttons promote the offer and drive traffic to landing pages
- Landing pages with registration forms collect leads information
- Thank you pages or delivery emails deliver the digital assets

The concept can be illustrated graphically like this:

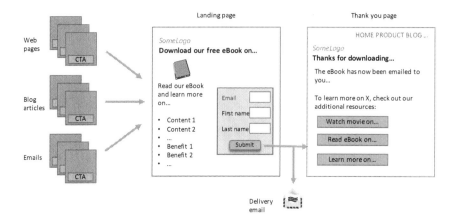

The beauty of it is that once you have it setup, it will run automatically, generating leads while you are abroad on holiday or mountain trekking on weekends. The system will relentlessly work for you day and night, generating more leads all the time. The only problem is, there is work for you to set this up in the first place.

To start with, you must have a digital asset or something else of desire to offer. A digital asset must have an educational or otherwise meaningful value. It can be a PDF document of some sort, a video tutorial, free evaluation versions of your software product, or your weekly stock market advice email.

When you have a desirable digital asset to offer (or something else, like free product samples), you can advertise it on your web pages, in blog articles, and in emails. The advertisement is done using a call-to-action (CTA) button. A CTA is just a clickable button or banner advertisement that promotes the offer to entice the visitor to click on it to get access to the offer.

Read our free eBook on Web Analytics!

26

Every web page on your website, every article on your blog, and every email you send should have at least one call-to-action button offering something. In short, take every opportunity you can to trigger your visitors to register their contact information.

For example, if a blog article is on French wines, you could include a call-to-action button offering a digital asset that relates to that topic. This could be an infographic map on the wine regions of France, or your eBook on the history of French winemaking. However, in your blog articles on cheese, you need a different digital asset that brings value to readers interested in that topic. Perhaps your weekly cheese tasting report will interest them, or your cheese making recipe eBook.

It is important your offers provide genuine value to your visitors, and that they relate to the topic of the web page or blog post that promotes them. If you search for "Italian sports cars" and find a blog article on the subject, it is not likely a call-to-action button offering an eBook on cooking triggers a click, right?

A click on a call-to-action button should open the landing page. The landing page has one purpose only: to make the visitor fill in their contact information in a registration form and click on a "Submit" button. To that end, the landing page should have no distracting options (like a navigation menu) that can make the visitor do something else and abandon the process.

Once the visitor has filled in the contact information and submitted the registration form, they are automatically redirected to a thank you page confirming the transaction. Now that you have the contact details, the game is reversed. The thank you page should be designed to keep the visitor on the website longer. Therefore, it should contain navigation controls, links to related reading on your website, and additional call-to-action buttons offering more educational content.

Through all this, do not fail to keep your part of the business deal. The visitor gave you the contact information, and now you must give him or her the digital asset. This can be done by sending an automatic delivery email with a download link, or by publishing the download link right on the thank you page.

Now, let's go into more detail and learn how to design effective call-to-action buttons, landing pages, registration forms, and thank you pages. They should all be optimized to collect as many leads as possible. The following sections outline best practices for this, and the next chapter covers how to create various types of digital marketing assets and how to optimize them for the best marketing results.

Call-to-action (CTA) buttons

Call-to-action buttons are fundamental to converting as many anonymous visitors as possible into leads. The CTA promotes your offer and is the first step of the leads conversion process. Call-to-action buttons can promote anything, and can be placed in any of your digital content including web pages, blog articles, emails, PDF files, and thank you pages.

Almost every web page, blog post, email, or PDF document you create should contain at least one call-to-action button that entices the reader to visit a landing page and register. Take every possible opportunity to add call-to-action buttons that promote your digital assets or other offers. A web page, blog post, email, or PDF document without a call-to-action button is a lost opportunity. Without the contact information, you cannot do any proactive marketing to your visitors.

The difference between a good call-to-action button and a poor one is what click-through rate it achieves. A well-designed call-to-action button can trigger many visitors to click on it, while an ineffective one doesn't. If visitors don't click on the CTA, they will never see the landing page with the registration form. To collect as many leads as possible, you need to have a great call-to-action button with a high click-through rate.

It is easy to add a call-to-action button somewhere as an after-thought at the end, but the better approach is to reverse the process. Before your write a new blog post or mailshot, consider what the next step is in the reader's customer journey. Then you can optimize the copy of the blog article or email so it leads up to the CTA button. This makes the reader want more information on the subject and increases the likelihood he or she will engage further.

Usually, the destination page of a call-to-action button is a dedicated landing page, with access to the digital asset guarded by a registration form. Make sure clicking on the CTA button opens the landing page in a new web browser window, rather than moving the visitor from the original page to the landing page in the same browser window. Why? There are two reasons.

First, if the visitor doesn't like the landing page or its offer, he or she will close the browser window to get rid of it. Unless the call-to-action button opens the landing page in a new window, you have also lost the visitor from your website if this happens. By letting call-to-action buttons open landing pages in new browser windows, you keep them on your website should they close the landing page window. At least you get a second chance to keep their interest.

Second, landing pages should be focused on the one and only goal of getting the visitor to submit the registration form. Hence, landing pages should have no navigation menus or other distracting content. This is hard to achieve if the landing page lives in the regular website window, as the website template likely adds menus and other distracting elements to all pages.

The title and other text on the call-to-action button should be short, with a clear message, and written in an actionable language. In practice, this means the title should start with a verb, like "Download...", "Request", "Read...", "Watch...", or "Learn..." It should also explain what the offer is and include relevant keywords. Try to be as clear and concise as possible.

The call-to-action button must stand out graphically, and should be relatively large without dominating the design. You want it in contrast (signal) colors, but you also want the coloring to work well with the visual scheme of your website.

A call-to-action button is a clickable hyperlink and must, therefore, look like a clickable object. Often this means it graphically looks like a button, but it can also look more like a banner advertisement. A call-to-action button that looks like a well-designed banner-ad will likely get a higher click-through rate than one that just looks like a text button.

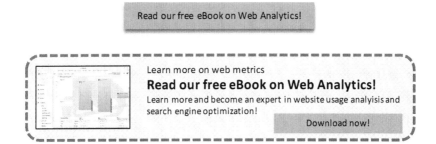

A text button can be implemented using HTML with CSS styling, or using a bitmap image. A graphical banner ad usually combines text and graphics inside the bitmap, as well as a region within the banner ad that looks like a clickable button. This is technically not the case, since the full image is the clickable area, not just the part of it that looks like a button. You can make it look more like a clickable object by adding rounded corners, 3D borders, and shading.

A recent trick to increase click-through rates is to add an arrow pointing to the call-to-action button. The arrow is annotated with a label along the lines of "Click here" or "Get the eBook". This can help draw more clicks.

Click here!

To create images implementing your call-to-action buttons, you can either use a bitmap editor like Adobe Photoshop (commercial) or GIMP (free). Perhaps easier, just use Microsoft PowerPoint or Apple Keynote and save the graphics as a bitmap image. There are also many button builder services on the Internet you can find with a search for "button generator".

Now that we know how to design call-to-action buttons, where should they be located for highest click-through rate? First, a call-to-action button should only be placed on a web page or in an email with content relevant to the offer it promotes. A call-to-action button advertising a motor yacht buyer's guide may not perform well on a web page on windsurfing, for example. Create another digital asset relevant to the web page and promote that instead of adding out-of-place offers.

Second, the call-to-action should be visible above the fold (i.e. without any need to scroll down to see it). Additional call-to-action buttons can be added below the fold, but make sure at least one of them is visible without scrolling. The exception is blog articles, where it makes the most sense to have the call-to-action button at the end of the article. The thinking here is that the blog article text leads up to the CTA offer.

The top left part of a web browser window is the area Internet users see first, so you may want to put your call-to-action button in that region. But this is not always possible, as the call-to-action button must also be located close to the content discussing the topic related to the offer. Make sure there is some white space around the CTA to make it look like an independent object, but don't put it too far away from the text that relates to it either, as it may become visually disconnected.

Landing pages

Along with call-to-action buttons that promote the offer, landing pages and the registration forms on them are the remaining parts that make or break the collection of contact information. This is a good example, although I would have used a contrast color for the Submit button:

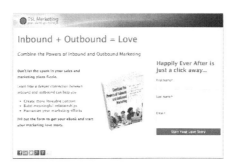

Each landing page is dedicated to just one task: to offer a particular digital asset and deliver it in return for contact information. Make sure there are no distractions that can make the visitor catch interest in anything else.

There should be no navigational controls whatsoever on a landing page, and this is why they often open in a new browser window outside of the regular website. This means the landing page has no menus and no other types of clickable links. There should be only one thing to do on the landing page: to fill in the registration form and click on that clearly visible submit button.

Make sure all content on the landing page is above the fold. Your visitors should not have to scroll down to see all of it. Remember, you want to reduce all distractions that may cause the visitor to lose interest and leave the landing page without registering their contact information.

All landing pages follow the same concept. They contain a company logo, a header, an image or photo, the body text, and a registration form with a highly visible submit button. Perhaps they include social sharing buttons too (this is the only distraction that is allowed).

The page header should clearly explain what is offered in an easy to comprehend manner. You don't have many seconds to keep the interest of the visitor. The language should be actionable, such as "Download our eBook on Windsurfing". If you need to say more in the header, add a sub-header like "A beginners guide to windsurfing".

Place a relevant graphic under the title, and make sure it relates to the offer. Is it an eBook or some other document? Add an image of the book. Since it is unlikely you have the physical book available in print to take a photo, create a virtual image of it. There are many services on the Internet offering 3D book cover image generation. Search for "free 3D book cover generator" to find some options, or take a screenshot of the first page of the document and use that to create a thumbnail image.

Below the header and image, provide the text outlining the content of the digital asset offered and the benefits of registering to download it. The copy should only be a couple of paragraphs of text describing what the offer is or contains, and a couple of paragraphs outlining how the offer will benefit the visitor (the value). Use bullet points highlighting the main value proposition and use boldface to highlight important keywords. Help the visitor to make a decision to register quickly; do not write too much text that can delay the "I will submit" decision.

At the bottom of the landing page, you can add social sharing buttons, with the hope visitors will spread the word of your offer. This is the only exception to the rule of not having any distracting elements on the landing page. It is worth the tradeoff if your landing page is shared on social media, as this can attract more visitors.

With the header and body text written in a compelling way to attract interest, and a beautiful image to further entice visitors, you need to add a registration form to collect contact details.

Registration forms

Registration forms are where the leads information is collected, and usually live in landing pages. Sometimes, registration forms live embedded in normal web pages or in blog articles too, but this is usually for simple forms, such as asking for an email address only. Registration forms can also exist in other shapes, for example pop-up or fly-out windows requesting visitors to fill in their email address when they arrive to the page. These are a bit more aggressive and intrusive.

Most often, the form stores the captured data in a leads database for further use later. This is the best way of recording the data unless you don't have a large number of leads. If this is the case, a simpler solution might be to have the form send you an email with the submitted information. Content management systems like WordPress or Joomla have numerous plug-ins that support these options, and marketing automation systems provide even better solutions.

How many question fields should a form have? You clearly want to know a lot more than basic contact information. If you run a sports equipment web shop, you will benefit from knowing what type of sport interests this lead. If you are in the software business, you may want to know if the visitor uses a Windows PC or Apple computer. A yoga club may want to know what type of classes the person is interested in. Companies selling complex and expensive software solutions may want to know the timeframe to start the deployment, and the work title of the lead.

Every business has its own set of questions to help segment the leads into different profiles or buyer personas. You can provide more relevant marketing content to the lead if you know more about them and their interests. The visitor, on the other hand, would prefer to give you no information at all. In reality, this boils down to having an acceptable balance between your desire for more information and the visitor's wish to give out as little as possible.

In general, you should only ask a minimum number of questions (one to three fields) if the digital asset is of relatively small value, such as a one-page infographic or registering for your monthly newsletter email. If the offer is of high value, such as free software, a training webinar, or a consultation, you can ask ten questions or so. For medium-value offers, such as eBooks, video tutorials, or white papers, perhaps five to seven fields are acceptable.

Remember, the more fields you have in the registration form, a larger share of visitors will abandon the process and exit the landing page without registering. You need to find the right balance. Form fields that are usually mandatory are the email address and often the first and last name. After that, the list of questions is highly dependent on your business.

You can use the number of form field questions to your benefit. Do you want more leads, even if they are of low quality? Use a smaller number of form field questions to reduce the bar. If you are already drenched in low-quality leads, you can add more form fields to scare off those with the least interest. People with a genuine and strong interest usually accept answering more questions than people with a marginal interest.

A final note on the form's Submit button. This should be the only clickable object on the landing page (except social media sharing buttons), since you want everything optimized for the one and only goal of getting the visitor to click on it. The Submit button should stand out visually by using a contrast color. Ideally, the default button text "Submit" is not the most effective. Instead, use a button text that explains what will happen in actionable language. Examples include "Download Now" or "Download the eBook".

How is a registration form created and added to a landing page? How does it store the captured contact information in a database? And how do I get the delivery email to be sent automatically once the Submit button is clicked?

These are all excellent questions and unfortunately, not so easy to answer. It depends on your website technology platform. If you use a content management system like WordPress or Joomla, there are plug-ins that can add this type of functionality. If your website runs on a basic web server without the ecosystem of a content management system, you are out of luck and you will have to build this logic yourself using HTML/JavaScript/SQL. Alternatively, try to find a dedicated landing page builder and hosting solution that enables you to create the landing pages with registration forms easily using their site. Many email service suppliers offer this feature, for example Campaign Monitor, GetResponse, MailChimp or AWeber.

The best way by far is to have a fully integrated marketing automation system like HubSpot, SalesForce Pardot, or Marketo. Marketing automation systems offers a fully integrated approach to almost everything related to online marketing, including call-to-action buttons, landing pages, registration forms, leads databases, emailing, and much more. The capabilities of modern marketing automation systems will be covered later.

Thank you pages

Thank you pages end the leads conversion process. Once the visitor has submitted the landing page registration form, two things needs to happen:

- You must deliver the digital asset offered on the landing page
- You must give the visitor a visual update indicating the "transaction" was successful

This is handled by thank you pages. After the Submit button has been clicked on a landing page registration form, the visitor should automatically be redirected to a thank you page. This gives the lead a visual update confirming the form submission went well. It also provides an opportunity to thank them for their interest in your offering and to make it available for immediate download.

However, the thank you page is also a perfect opportunity to direct the new lead to further information by adding more call-to-action buttons promoting additional content, with the hope of engaging a bit longer. So what does a good thank you page look like?

First, you can return the navigation controls. You now have the contact information and can relax a little bit. You also want the new lead to continue browsing for more information on your website. Adding menus and other navigation controls will help. You must also deliver the offer promoted by the landing page.

There are two options:

- Have the digital asset available for immediate download on the thank you page
- Send an automatic email delivering the digital asset

The first option is the most natural, is easiest to set up for you, and is most convenient for your leads. The problem is that this setup allows visitors to get access to your digital asset by entering fake or non-existent email addresses.

The other option is to send an automatic email with the download link. This is more cumbersome to setup and is more inconvenient to the lead, as there may be a delay before the email arrives, or it may be stopped by spam filters. However, at least you know you will get a working email address.

It is up to you which one to choose, but I tend to prefer the second one as it gives me working email addresses, even though it is more complicated to setup. This solution does not help against temporary email addresses, of course, so it is not bulletproof either.

If you are on social media like Facebook, LinkedIn, or Twitter, add social sharing buttons to the thank you page to make it easy for the new lead to share the offer on the recently downloaded digital asset to his or her friends.

Chapter summary

This chapter focused on how to convert anonymous visitors into identified leads, using call-to-action buttons for promotion of desirable digital assets, landing pages with registration forms for leads capture, and thank you pages and delivery emails for content distribution.

The next chapter details what digital assets you can create to entice visitors to give you their contact information, along with best practices in how to create them.

Content creation and digital assets

To convert anonymous visitors into leads you can start to nurture and follow-up with, you will have to get their contact information. The previous chapter outlined how to turn anonymous visitors into identified leads by offering digital assets in return for a visitor's contact details. Landing pages with registration forms were used to capture the data and thank you pages or delivery emails were used to distribute the requested digital asset on offer.

So what digital assets do visitors want badly enough to give you their contact information? There are many types of resources that are valuable enough to trigger the conversion. Typically, this is a digital document of some form. The digital assets can be things like PDF documents. Other types of digital assets are Microsoft PowerPoint or Apple Keynote presentations, document templates of various kinds, sound or video files, and free photo or image libraries.

Other types of offers can also be used for leads conversion. This includes seminar or webinar registrations, free downloads of demo software, offers for free consultations, signing up for weekly stock market advice emails, or free product samples.

Different types of digital content are better suited at various steps in the marketing funnel and customer journey. Before you create digital content, you need to know where it maps in these processes. Early in the buyer's journey, you should offer educational and problem-solving assets. In the middle, provide more product oriented information, and at the end use comparative or relationship building assets like buyer's guides, case studies, webinars, or free consultations.

Always consider the type of content and format the user needs that fit with the optimized buyer personas and search keywords.

Tools for content creation

Digital content usually consists of text and graphics, but can also be other things like audio, video, or software products. So what tools are used to create the content?

Text is most easily written in Microsoft Word or Apple Pages. If you are like most people, you might be scared your grammar or spelling is not perfect enough for publishing to the general public. While you can use the built-in spell and grammar checker of your word processing software, there are more capable solutions available.

Grammarly, for example, provides a spell and grammar checker with a generic web interface as well as Microsoft Word and Microsoft Outlook integration. It also detects plagiarism, immediately flagging your text if it's found to have been copied from another site. Search for "Grammar checking" and you will find additional products from other vendors.

Graphics can be created or altered in image editing software like Adobe Photoshop or GIMP. In my opinion, presentation software tools like Microsoft PowerPoint or Apple Keynote are vastly underestimated for graphic creation. Banner ads, call-to-action buttons, graphical illustrations for eBooks or blog articles, and more can easily be created in this type of presentation software.

For audio recording and editing, Apple's GarageBand (available on Apple platforms), Audacity (free of charge and available on both Mac and Windows), or Adobe Audition (a professional-grade solution) all work.

You can use Apple iMovie or Microsoft Movie Maker for video editing. Many marketing videos include recorded screen captures—use a dedicated screen recording solution like Camtasia or Cam Studio for this.

Infographics

Infographics are easily consumed and understood graphical representations of information. They should be educational and entertaining, and not contain a strong sales message. Position yourself as a leading source of useful information in your market, and leads and customers will eventually find you themselves.

Since infographics are a visual presentation of information, you need to gather the data before you start. Make sure it is credible and accurate—you don't want to distribute erroneous information.

With the data assembled, the second step is to draw a wireframe using a pencil and paper. That way you can quickly sketch and scrap a few iterations before you end up with a graphical concept you like. Try to present a clear story in a logical manner and with a natural flow. Also, make sure the tone fits the purpose. An infographic on deadly diseases may not benefit from humor, while one on movie stars may well do.

Use visual elements to make the infographics more attractive and try to think a little bit outside the box. A donut or radar chart may be more interesting than a bar graph, and a thermometer scale may be more interesting than just a number. In addition to graphical charts, many other types of graphics can enrich your layout.

Place some bottles, cars, hamburgers, or people next to each other to visually show that there is more of one thing than another. You could also use a map annotated with text bubbles of information. Flowcharts make great infographic elements, as do various types of dashboard objects. Do an image search on Google for "infographics elements" or "infographics objects" for more ideas.

Typefaces (fonts) should be consistent, or at least complement each other, and don't make them steal attention from the graphics. You may want to align the colors to your corporate graphical profile if you have any. At least make sure to use the same color scheme as your website uses. Break up information and try to avoid information overload. Make use of white space for the best effect.

If you want a ready-made infographics example you can use, search for "infographics template" for many good readymade templates. There are also a large number of infographics generation tools available on the Internet. Search for "infographics generator" to get started.

If you have reasonably good eyes for graphic design, Microsoft PowerPoint is a useful tool for infographics creation. You can assemble different graphical objects like rectangles, circles, block arrows, flowchart symbols, clipart graphics, and talk bubbles in PowerPoint. Then make them more attractive by modifying background and border colors, adding gradient fills and dashed borders or 3D shadows, or connect them with arrows.

SmartArt in Microsoft PowerPoint allows you to create visually rich representations of data, such as adding layers to a pyramid, creating a ring of circles, and more. SmartArt adds or removes graphical items to the object depending on how many text items you add to its text outline, which defines what labels should go into the illustration.

Using the "Save As" option in Microsoft PowerPoint, you can save the slide as a PNG file. It can then be added to a web page, a Word document, or to an email.

Infographics make great digital assets that you can protected behind landing page web forms, provided they present information of enough value.

eBooks

An eBook is a digital offer of perceived high value. It should be educational, not product-focused, although you may mention your product. When you hear the term eBook, you may think about a 50-200 page formal document written in Microsoft Word or Apple Pages. If that were the case, writing them would be a huge undertaking, and your visitors would not have time to read them. Realistically, they are probably too boring to read too.

A successful eBook (in the context of a digital asset for marketing purposes) is often a spacious and graphically rich Microsoft PowerPoint or Apple Keynote presentation. It is often 10-20 pages or so, and designed to look like a non-fiction book with a medium text density. Search for "eBook template" for plenty of examples.

Before writing the eBook, you should carefully consider who the intended readers are, as you need to make sure the content matches their interests, pain points, and needs. Spend some time thinking about what title will attract the most downloads. You want the title to be both enticing and descriptive.

The eBook needs to contain a graphical cover page, a table of contents, a chapter front page, and a few body pages for each chapter. It should also have a final page with a call-to-action message requesting the reader take the next step in the buyer's journey. Other pages may also contain calls-to-action of course, as long as they are not too pushy that they devalue the rest of the book.

If you design the eBook in Microsoft PowerPoint or Apple Keynote, you can quickly add text boxes and other graphical objects, apply colors, drop shadows, and more. Adding a quote in a sidebar with larger text font adds to the interest, as well as adding charts or infographics.

For your eBook to have working calls-to-action, prompting the reader to take further actions, you need to make text or graphics clickable by adding hyperlinks. If you are on social media, you shall also add clickable social sharing buttons to the header or footer of the eBook.

You can add clickable hyperlinks with Microsoft PowerPoint. After saving the eBook into PDF format, these call-to-action or social sharing hyperlinks should be clickable, driving the reader to whatever landing page or resource you promote as the next step in the customer journey.

White papers

A white paper is an in-depth technical report on a particular problem that provides a solution. It should be technology focused, and not really mention products.

A white paper is a high-value digital asset that should educate the reader, and product promotion may not be welcomed. They are used for thought leadership, trust generation, and leads education, and are great for leads generation due to their high perceived value. A white paper is the academic research report of marketing documents, so to speak.

A white paper is often between 10-30 pages, but can be much longer. Hence, they are relatively demanding to develop. They are formal documents that typically start by defining and discussing the problem, before moving on to provide the solution. They have a much higher text density than eBooks and should be written in a professional and serious writing style.

Document and formula templates

Would your potential customers have a use for any Microsoft Word, Excel, PowerPoint, or other software templates? In many industries, your potential customers may need to create documents in a particular format. Help them by offering readymade examples for free. They will remember where they got the template.

If you sell book-publishing services, perhaps you can offer free Word templates for good-looking books? Do you sell software development tools? Provide Word templates for documents typically produced by software development teams like software requirements specifications, interface specifications, and software test descriptions. Do you sell clothing for bird watchers? Provide a Word document template where bird sightings can be registered and archived.

In many cases, Excel sheets can be useful too. Do you sell scuba diving equipment? Offer a Microsoft Excel formula template that calculates safe dive times and provides a dive log. Do you sell equipment to soccer clubs? Offer a soccer tournament template. Do you sell stock market advice? Provide Excel formulas to document trading strategies, trading logs, or the like.

PowerPoint templates may be less useful to offer (other than just graphical templates), but perhaps you can find some useful options. If you sell equipment to sailing clubs, for example, offer a ready-made PowerPoint template containing nicely designed graphical elements to help visualize the race course map (for the planning meetings prior to the race), or maybe a template for presenting the race results.

Do potential customers in your industry fill in forms of any type? Create ready-made templates in Word, Excel, or PowerPoint as appropriate.

Checklists

Knowledge can often be shared using checklists that summarize the most important steps with a short description of some activity in a few clear and concise steps. A checklist is typically a bulleted or numbered list of items to achieve a particular goal. It may be one page only, or contain a bit more information spread over a few pages.

Some examples are:

- Do you offer website design services? Offer a checklist potential customers can read to learn what preparations they should do before starting a new website project.

- Do you sell mountain trekking gear? Provide a checklist highlighting what preparations and equipment are needed for a mountain adventure.

- Do you sell landscaping services? Offer a checklist with the most important steps in garden planning.

- Do you sell photography equipment or training classes? Provide a checklist of the steps needed to help ensure they take a good quality photo.

You get the idea.

Presentations

You probably have many PowerPoint presentations already made. Why not use them as digital assets too? Perhaps you can use them as-is, or massage them a little into educational content of value to your website or blog visitors. In particular, PowerPoint presentations made for training or informational purposes make great digital assets that can be fenced behind a landing page. Your product sales presentation is probably not as useful here.

As always, make sure at least the final page includes a call-to-action button that advertises some additional offer, for example more educational white papers or eBooks. This helps drive more traffic back to your website.

Often you distribute the presentation in PDF format, as you don't want the distributed document to be editable (PDF files are increasingly becoming editable now too, but nevertheless). This is not a problem, as PDFs can now have clickable hyperlinks that make it possible to add working call-to-action buttons.

You can also publish your presentations on SlideShare, which becomes an additional channel for market visibility and leads generation. Using SlideShare, you can add leads capture forms to any page in the presentation, blocking further access until the form is filled in. SlideShare can also integrate with marketing automation systems, thus automatically transferring new leads into your main leads database.

Case studies

Case studies are great because they give endorsements from existing customers, thus creating a marketing message that is perceived to be more trustworthy than the usual sales collaterals many companies send out.

When creating a case study based on one of your existing customers, you should obviously select a customer with good product knowledge who has received good results from using your product. If you can, chose a customer with an impressive and well-known brand name, or a company who switched from your competitor's product to yours.

Make them feel special and ask them to be interviewed for a case study. Personal ego and the chance to get their name published can do wonders. When preparing for the case study, list some interview questions in advance. For example:

- What problems did they have before selecting your product?
- Why did they select your product?
- How did your product help solve the problems?
- What are the best capabilities of your product?
- How are their results better after using your product?
- What is the primary reason they can recommend your product?

When you have captured the interview answers, it is time to prepare the actual case study document. It should contain an executive summary, a description of the interviewed customer, the problems they had, and how your product solved them. If the improved results can be measured numerically, include this information.

Also include positive quotes from the interviewed customer and add to the case study (in several places if you got multiple quotes) and make sure to add a call-to-action on the final page. If you have a clickable hyperlink button on the last page, the reader may click on the CTA link and engage with you further.

Videos

Videos can be great digital assets published for public access on your website or blog, or on video sharing sites like YouTube and Vimeo for brand building or thought leadership. You can also gate high-value videos behind a landing page and use them as a leads generator. Emails can include videos too.

There are many types of videos you can publish, including educational or training videos, product demo videos, interviews, marketing videos, or testimonials from customers or partners. While videos may take an effort to develop, they are fun and interesting to view and can often help engage with your visitors and leads.

Some impressive capabilities can be provided on video sharing or hosting sites. YouTube, for example, supports video annotations allowing you to add text layers with clickable links on top of any part of a video. Use annotations to get subscribers to your YouTube channel or link to other content.

Video marketing platforms like Wistia and VidYard are becoming more popular and are more advanced than basic video hosting sites. Videos can now be gated without protecting them behind a landing page using in-video gating. This means the movie itself (or so it appears to the viewer) asks for an email address or something else before it plays, in the middle of the film, or at the end.

Video marketing platforms also provide marketing performance analysis, including features for understanding who watches the videos, where they are from, and with which operating system or device. Video marketing platforms allow you to add call-to-action buttons to movies, which can be added in-video or as popup windows. They also integrate with marketing automation systems and customer relationship management (CRM) software, automatically synchronizing contact information and video usage information of your leads between the systems.

Even if you don't make use of technologies like YouTube annotations, or the more advanced capabilities of video marketing platforms like Wistia or VidYard, make sure the film does not end with a black frame. Rather, end it with a call-to-action urging the viewer to engage with you a bit more.

Webinars

A webinar is like a physical seminar that has moved over to the Internet and is performed digitally as a virtual web-based event, instead of being run physically in a hotel or exhibition center.

Presenting at a webinar is much like talking to real people in front of you, except that you and all attendees attend using their computers. In short, you share the contents of your screen and your voice using a microphone, and the attendees see your screen and hear you live in real-time. Webinars have strong benefits, particularly if you are far away from your customers.

You can easily run a webinar with 12 attendees from London, 8 from Boston, 5 from San Francisco, and 2 from Japan, almost for free. The only difficulty in running global webinars might be the time zone difference, which is a small price to pay compared to having to fly to another country or continent to attend physical meetings.

When you plan and promote a webinar, make sure the title matches the intended audience or vice versa. You will not get many registrations if you send a webinar invitation to a segment of leads with entirely different interests. Make sure the intended audience understands the value of the webinar and always consider the buyer personas and segmentation of the list of leads you want to attract with it.

To be successful, a webinar needs to give information of real value, like sharing useful advice or knowledge. Do not just fill the webinar with buzzwords or sales fluff. Try to understand what expectations, pain points, and needs the intended attendees have. The better you match that, the happier attendees will be. That makes an excellent webinar success.

In addition to the presentation (often done in PowerPoint), it might be good to run a live demo of your product as well. If you sell software, a live demo using real-time screen capture/sharing makes great content in a webinar. If you have a physical product that can be demoed using a webcam at your desk, that can be a possibility too.

Do not make a webinar too long. Normally attendees get impatient after 30 minutes unless the knowledge you share is of high quality. Don't make it over an hour, unless it is web training with paying customers or something similar. Also, make sure it completes in the time frame presented in the invitation.

Like physical seminars with many real attendees showing up, webinars also require preparations. Your attendees expect the same quality presentation even if they watch it over the internet as they would if they were in front of you. You should expect that preparations for a good seminar take several hours, perhaps even tens of hours, depending on the complexity of your presentation and how much material you have readymade.

For example, you need to finalize the webinar title and abstract before you can start to promote the event. You will have to set up a landing page with a registration form to collect attendee registrations. Then advertise the webinar and registration page minimum a couple of weeks in advance. Use banner ads or call-to-action buttons on your website and blog, as well as well-targeted mailshots, social media outreach, paid ads, or offline marketing. You probably want to send a reminder email to registered attendees a few days prior to the event as well.

Some webinar software solutions allow you to prepare poll questions that can be asked using popup windows during the webinar. If so, plan these poll questions well in advance. Make sure the questions give valuable feedback to you and are not asked at random just because the capability is there.

You should not end the webinar without an offer promoting the next step in the customer journey. Offer a free demo, a free consultation, a free eBook, or something to set up the bait and make the attendee take the next step towards placing a purchase order.

Before running the webinar, test that the software and microphone works as expected. Ensure the webinar will be hosted from a quiet place—you do not want to be disturbed by aircraft landing nearby, your baby screaming in the next room, or loud phone calls. Make sure to disable any programs on your PC that may generate embarrassing pop-up notifications, like chat applications, Skype, email clients, or calendar reminders. You do not want a friend to remind you and all the attendees about all the tequilas you shared last weekend!

When running the webinar, try to use a friendly, casual, and conversational style, and do not read a script like a robot. If possible, record the webinar into a video file you can publish as a marketing asset later on. If you can, have a moderator managing the chat window and taking notes on attendee questions while the presenter focuses on running the webinar.

After the webinar, you should analyze the poll questions. If you recorded it, you can edit and polish it for publishing. Then promote it as a free on-demand training video. You can host it behind a landing page on your website (as a leads generator). Alternatively, publish it on a video sharing site like YouTube or Vimeo as a publicly available marketing resource (for brand awareness or attracting visitors to your website). Perhaps you can post the webinar Q&A's as a blog post along with an offer to watch the full recorded webinar.

Finally, follow-up with the attendees soon, asking for their feedback and if they have any additional questions they may want to be answered. If you do not have time to follow up manually, you can prepare a follow-up email in advance and send it to all attendees right after the webinar.

Professional but inexpensive webinar solutions include GotoWebinar from Citrix and WebEx from Cisco.

A good webinar solution can include features like:

- Webinar and webinar series scheduling
- Registration page and attendee management
- Voice over IP internet sound or local dial-in from landlines in various countries

- Distribution of webinar invitation emails with login information
- Screen sharing, either full screen or just a selected window
- Drawing tools, allowing you to sketch on the webinar screen to highlight certain areas you talk about
- Recording of the webinar
- Chat window
- Possibility to mute attendees for anti-echo or other reasons
- Poll questions popping up during the webinar for participants to respond to
- Webinar attendee behavior and poll question analytics
- Attendee feedback surveys right after the webinar exits
- Integration with marketing automation systems

If your webinar solution does not offer recording, a separate and independent screen recording solution like Camtasia may handle this. You can also search for "screen recorder" to find multiple software options. However, a separate screen recorder solution may have the drawback of notifications from attendee chat messages or other unsuitable popups shown in the recorded movie. Also, basic screen sharing software does of course not have all the nice webinar-specific capabilities listed above.

Podcasts

Podcasts are feeds of on-demand audio you can download from the Internet and listen to while in the car, jogging, or sunbathing at the beach. Offering podcasts is another medium you can use to reach your target audience.

Since podcasts are feeds publishing new talk show episodes over time, they contain many episodes. This can, for example, be a weekly industry news wrap-up, cooking advice, or stock market analysis. People subscribe to the podcast, and a smartphone app automatically downloads all new episodes as they become available.

Edison Research reports over 45 million Americans listen to podcasts regularly. This is quite a lot, and one likely reason for their quick adoption is the ease-of-use with smartphones. For example, the Apple iPhone has a podcast app built-in.

A podcast episode is generally a talk show in which a host invites guests to have a discussion on something related to the topic. The podcast itself can be created using a sound recording and editing tool like Apple's GarageBand, Audacity, or Adobe Audition.

You will also need a high-quality microphone and a quiet room to record in. If you want to interview people remotely, you can use Skype, which allows recording the phone call using an add-on.

When produced, you need to publish the podcast episode for your audience. Since a podcast is a feed, there are some mechanics involved in setting it up in a way podcast-listening apps can understand. A podcast is not just uploading an MP3 file to your website. To be a podcast, the recordings need to be a feed of episodes, published in a format the podcast listening apps interpret.

You could publish the podcast feed yourself, but it is easier to host it on a sound hosting platform like SoundCloud. With these services, all you need to do is to upload the audio file and all the feed mechanics are handled automatically. Once the feed is operational, you can register the podcast with Apple iTunes.

With a podcast going live, there is still no guarantee for success. You will have to promote it through the website, the blog, or using social media and email. Perhaps you can do cross-promotion with other websites and have them promote it too. As always, quality content is king. No one wants to listen to rubbish. Make sure the podcast discusses topics of real use and value for your intended audience.

Chapter summary

In this chapter, we discussed what tools can be used to create digital assets, along with best practice for creating them. There are many different types of digital assets that can be used, including infographics, eBooks, and white papers. The next chapter provides information on how to increase the interest level of the leads you have captured.

Email marketing

Thanks to other marketing efforts, you managed to attract new visitors to your website and convert them into leads. Now what? How can you make leads keep and increase their interest level until the timing is right for a purchase decision that may be weeks or months away?

You need to deploy leads nurturing techniques that make you stay on top of their minds, and make them engage with you more deeply over time as you continue to provide useful and valuable information. Leads nurturing is about growing the relationship and, done right, it increases trust and thought leadership.

In practice, online leads nurturing is about sending automatic marketing emails to your leads. There are two types of leads nurturing emails you can use:

- Mailshots (proactive leads nurturing). This means sending a large number of identical or similar emails to many leads at the same time. This happens relatively rarely and can be managed manually with the help of an emailing service provider. Think monthly newsletter emails or campaign mailshots here.

- Drip emails (reactive leads nurturing). This means sending a set of individual emails to a specific lead when a certain event has been triggered (such as a landing page form submission). This can happen at any time and cannot be done without software automation.

It wasn't too long ago that Internet marketers mostly used mailshots, often in the form of sending monthly newsletter emails to all the leads in the database. This strategy is often not the most effective one, although mailshots can still be useful if done right. Nowadays, more focus is put on reactive leads nurturing emails providing a more personalized experience, and most importantly, offering relevant information at the time the lead has an active interest in your offerings.

In either case, ask yourself if the email you plan to send is giving any value to your lead. If it doesn't, you are probably trying to sell your product too hard and are not following the principle of providing educational or otherwise valuable content that helps build trust and engagement.

Reactive leads nurturing

Reactive leads nurturing is about sending a series of associated emails with a coherent purpose as a result of a specific lead engaging with you in some way. Automated leads nurturing workflows should be initiated immediately when a lead interacts with you, for example when a visitor registers their contact information in a landing page form to get an eBook.

The leads nurturing workflow for that particular digital asset (the eBook) is triggered upon the form submission and may include sending additional emails on related topics during the next few days or weeks. The goal here is to push the lead further into the customer journey and closer to the sale by increasing the interest.

The nurturing emails should be short and relevant. Send no more than 5-7 emails in total, with some days or even a week or two between each one. The first email should be trust building, and explain why you contact them (they downloaded the digital asset) and offer additional educational or useful information (such as another eBook offer). Do not promote your product yet; the goal here is to make the lead trust you enough to open later emails too.

Send a couple more emails offering additional educational resources some days apart. Then you can send an email with a soft sales message, and later another with a harder sales message. At the end, if the lead has not responded to the sales offer emails, send one more explaining you will not send any more emails. This is the break-up message.

Always make sure the leads nurturing emails cover a topic similar to that of the action that triggered the start of the workflow.

For each digital asset you offer behind a landing page form, design and set up the leads nurturing workflow that should be started when the form is submitted. Ideally, each landing page form should have its own email workflow that is optimized to increase the interest level of a lead who downloaded that digital asset. The leads nurturing workflow could for example look like this:

| Trust building email | Educational offer 1 email | Educational offer 2 email | Soft sell email | Hard sell email | Break up email |

Marketing automation systems support designing workflows that can contain *if...then...else* logic. For example, you can design a workflow that does different things depending on how the lead reacts to your leads nurturing emails. If an email is not opened, you can send a reminder some days later. If an email contains two call-to-action buttons, the workflow can adapt its remaining behavior based on which one was clicked.

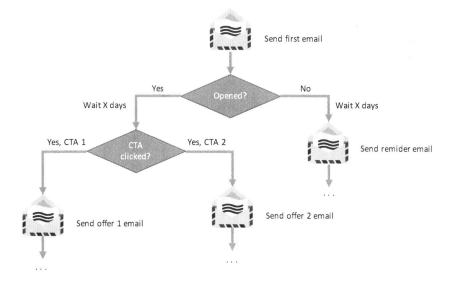

Proactive leads nurturing

Mass mailshots are not dead yet. In fact, they can be highly effective if done properly. They allow you to communicate product or company news, offers, or discount campaigns as needed. However, if done wrong they are a big turn-off for many people. In particular, monthly newsletters may not be the best way. Read the next section for more details on newsletter emails.

The trick is to send your mailshots to better-segmented address lists, such that you send only relevant information to certain groups of your leads database. It is unlikely the same email sent to all your leads will feel equally relevant to all of them. Doing that only makes you appear spammy and does nothing to help increase the engagement level.

Make an effort to ensure all leads get an email covering a subject that is likely to feel valuable and useful to them. Scale back on the same mailshots sent to everyone and instead try to send better-targeted emails to different groups of leads. A short and concise email with a focused goal (such as offering your new free eBook on windsurfing) can still be effective if it is sent to leads with a particular interest in that subject. Other leads in your database (who are interested in speedboats) may find the same email to be spam.

You should also segment the email recipients by stage in the marketing funnel if you can. New leads, for example, should receive email offers on more educational and problem-solving content to increase trust and thought leadership. For leads that are further into the buyer's journey and more likely to buy your product or service soon, you might be better served by promoting comparative assets. This can be documents like buyer's guides, case studies, or discount offers.

Newsletter emails

As you have surely noticed, many companies send email newsletters with irrelevant or un-engaging content to poorly segmented lists. This only results in low open and click-through rates, and many unsubscribes. The result? A poor reputation score from the intended audience. Perhaps even worse, you can get a lower sender score that may affect your future email delivery success (we'll cover this in the next section).

An email newsletter is not a dedicated marketing message that promotes one event or one offer, a transactional delivery email, a reactive leads nurturing email, or a monthly round up of your latest blog articles. Rather, it is a general email containing a mix of company, product, or event news, educational content, or promotions. Additionally, newsletter emails are usually not sent to a focused segment of the leads database, but to all leads.

While newsletter emails are one of the most common types of emails, they have a difficult time catching the reader's interest. This is because they have such unfocused content, and hence both open and click-through rates may be low. It may be difficult to reach success with general repetitive newsletter emails nowadays, but there are some advantages. One of the better ones is brand awareness and making sure customers don't forget about you.

If you decide you still want to run newsletter emails, try to make sure the majority of the message is of educational content, and only a small part is promotional. Even if readers like your company, they may lose interest if they only get a sales pitch for your product all the time. Eventually, they will unsubscribe if you don't give them truly valuable and useful information.

Only promote it when you have real product news of considerable relevance. Otherwise, try to provide educational content of value to the reader instead.

In a newsletter with several articles of unrelated materials, probably each with its call-to-action button, it is easy for the reader to get distracted and not click on a call-to-action button at all. My recommendation is to have one big call-to-action for the most important piece of information in the newsletter, and make the other less prioritized call-to-action buttons smaller and less prominent. That way, readers are more likely to click the most important one while the others are available as a second option.

A newsletter email with several different stories might look complex. Therefore, try to keep the texts short and concise, with a not-too-busy layout, and with a lot of white space to calm things down.

As many email clients block downloading email images, it is a good idea to enter the ALT text that is shown instead of the image if disabled. That way, the reader can at least read a piece of text that explains which photo should have been there.

If your emailing platform supports measuring email opens and click-through rates (it should!), pay attention to these numbers. They can provide useful information, for example if your open rates are dropping dramatically with each mailshot. Analyzing and comparing the open and click-through rates of several emails also gives you a hint on what type of content is most successful with your leads.

You can easily measure click-through rates using a good mailing platform (this is accurately tracked using URL redirects), but the open rates are more difficult to trust. The reason is that you can only measure if an email has been opened or not using a trick that involves a very small (often 1x1 pixel) image with transparent color being added to the email layout. If someone opens your message, the email client downloads the invisible image, which can be tracked on the webserver storing it.

As mentioned, many email clients have image downloads disabled, and in such case, the image isn't downloaded even if the email is opened. Email clients may also have an automatic preview of the HTML layout. In such case, the image is downloaded even if the recipient didn't open or read the email. While it is important to track also the open rates, be aware this figure is not 100% accurate.

Sending email

In addition to websites, email was the first Internet medium used for marketing. Unfortunately, email has been massively misused and the majority of all emails sent are spam. Kaspersky Labs reports over 65% of all email is spam, and some months it surpasses 70%.

To be successful, you must ensure you are a trustworthy sender, and your emails must be engaging and relevant to the readers. Even if recipients don't spam flag your emails or unsubscribe from your mailing list, they may have mentally unsubscribed, and delete your emails without reading them.

So what are the best practices for sending marketing emails? Before doing so on a larger scale, you need to consider some important topics:

- Legal issues
- Different opt-in types
- Deliverability rate and spam filters
- Open rates
- Click-through rates
- Spam flagging and unregister rates

All emails you send need to be delivered, opened, and have a click-through to achieve its goal of pushing the lead closer to the sale. It should not trigger the recipient to unregister or spam-flag the email. It goes without saying that you should not violate applicable marketing and spam laws either.

Legal issues

You have to consider legal issues related to marketing email and spam. In the United States for example, the CAN-SPAM-Act is the governing law. Similarly, Australia has its Spam Act, Canada has the Canadian Anti-Spam Law (CASL), and in Europe, a European Directive covers marketing emails. Other countries have their own laws.

You can read this page for more information on spam legislation in different countries:

https://en.wikipedia.org/wiki/Email_spam_legislation_by_ country

Please note that I take no legal responsibility for any of the information in this book. Always consult an authorized legal advisor in case of doubt. A good start in complying with the law is to make sure you only send email to people who have properly opted-in.

Opt-in strategies

There are different strategies for collecting email addresses. Obviously, you should never buy any address list or gather email addresses using other questionable means. Only collect the email addresses of people who have voluntarily given it to you, and never send emails to people who do not expect you to do so. That makes you a spammer, and it may be illegal as well.

Once you have captured an email address in a registration form, you can use different opt-in strategies to qualify it:

- Single opt-in
- Single opt-in with a welcome email
- Double opt-in

With single opt-in, you just capture the email address in a form and start to use it at a later time. You can optionally use a "Send marketing information" checkbox to give the visitor the chance to decide whether to accept marketing emails. The advantage with single opt-in is you get more email addresses with a minimum of fuss. The disadvantage is illegitimate email addresses may be entered (for example by spambots), causing you to send emails to unhappy recipients or spamtraps.

Single opt-in with a welcome mail works the same, but a welcome letter is automatically sent upon registration, setting the expectation for what types of emails the reader can expect in the future. An advantage is that the welcome email can include call-to-action buttons promoting offers for more content, which can increase engagement.

With double opt-in, an email is sent to the recipient when they submit the form. This email requests the reader to confirm he or she really wants to register to the mailing list by clicking a link in the email. The email address is not added to the mailing list before this confirmation has been done. With double opt-in, the quality of your address list becomes higher and email addresses submitted by spambots are not used, but you may lose some interested subscribers who do not bother to take the extra step.

What about email addresses you collect in real life? For example, attendees to events you sponsor, business cards collected at a trade exhibition, or in business meetings? Marketing emails may not be welcome just because you got someone's business card. An email is spam if the receiver does not expect and welcome it, even if you feel differently. In my opinion, the best approach here is to send a personal email from your own email address, acknowledging how you met and ask them to add themselves to your mailing list. Add a link to the registration form in your email to make it easy for them to sign up.

Deliverability and spam filters

It cannot be emphasized enough that you should only send marketing emails to people who have opted-in properly. Again, never buy a list of email addresses and send mail blasts to them—they don't want to hear from you.

Sending email to purchased email lists makes you a spammer. It also reduces your brand goodwill and trustworthiness, and the receivers are likely to spam-flag your email. Furthermore, your company will get a lower spam reputation on the Internet, which actually hurts your email deliverability even for legitimate email. In short, you piss people off, and you hurt your delivery rate for email to people who have opted-in. It may be illegal too.

The right way to do it is to entice website and blog visitors enough to make them opt-in, thanks to the thought leadership and helpful content you offer them. That way, you will grow your email list with people who are eager to hear from you.

Unfortunately, your address list becomes less useful over time. It is normal to expect 20% or more of the email addresses to become worthless each year. This is because recipients unregister, leave the company they work for, or the company may go out of business.

Thus, when you send mailshots, many of the email addresses may not work any longer. When an email can't be delivered, you get a bounce. A hard bounce happens when the email address doesn't work due to a more permanent reason, for example the email address or the company may no longer exist. A soft bounce happens when the email couldn't be delivered this time, likely due to a more temporary problem. For example, the inbox of the recipient may be full or the email may contain attachments that are too large.

Assuming you have a high-quality email list in place, how do you get your emails delivered rather than ending up in spam filters? First, remove hard-bounced email addresses from the mailing list—a good mailing service provider will do this automatically. Resending to nonexistent email addresses is not good practice, and can harm your spam reputation.

Another problem is spamtraps. These are email addresses created with the purpose of detecting spammers. The email address was likely never promoted or used, but may still receive an email, thus flagging the sender as a spammer.

The sender may have sent a large amount of emails using a software program to auto-generate random email addresses, or websites are seeded with spamtrap email addresses, and someone scraped them from such a website. Furthermore, an internet service provider (ISP) may consider incoming email to be spam if the mail account has been inactive for a year or more.

Since you are not a spammer, you may think you don't need to worry about this. However, you may run into problems unless you have double opt-in email forms, as other people or spambots may enter spamtrap email addresses into your registration forms. You then appear to be a spammer, which can seriously harm your reputation.

Mail servers are rated with a sender score, which is the spam reputation of your email server. The sender score is calculated for each outgoing email server's IP address in the range from 0 (bad) to 100 (good). If your score is over 90, you are doing well. If your score is between 50 and 85, your score is not as good as it should be, and if it is under 50, you have a problem. Scores are calculated using data from millions of mailboxes, and a company called Return Path manages it.

Your sender score changes over time, depending on how your recipients spam-flag your mailshots, and other reasons. In addition to the risk of getting a low sender score, your email server may be blacklisted. This is why it is so important to have only people who actively opted-in on your email list. Otherwise, you encounter a big risk of having a large part of all your emails being blocked by spam filters.

I strongly recommend you send marketing emails from a different server (i.e. different IP address) than your normal business emails. Keep an eye on your sender score. If it is too low, you need to reassess how you send marketing emails. You can check your sender score at **www.senderscore.org**.

Also, make sure there is an unsubscribe link in all emails you send, and that the opt-out is honored. Finally, take help from your email hosting supplier and ensure you have SPF and DKIM authentication set up for your outgoing email accounts (this is too technical to cover in this book).

Open rates

Having your emails delivered is a good start, but it doesn't help if your recipients do not open it and delete it immediately. So, open rates are the next important thing you need to worry about after deliverability. When recipients lose interest in your emails if they are unengaging or provide no value to them, they start to delete your emails instead of opening and reading them. Even if they do not unsubscribe, this this is a mental unsubscribe with the same effect. Your emails are not read.

Except the value perceived in previous emails, the most important thing in improving your open rates are the three things that are typically shown in the email client before an email is opened:

- Sender name
- Subject line
- Message preview

Make sure the sender name is recognizably related to your company such that they want to open it instead of thinking it is spam from someone else. In practice, your company name should be visible in the sender name, such as "From: MyCompany, Inc". However, practical statistics have shown that sender names including a personal touch increase the open rate. Perhaps something like "From: John Smith, MyCompany Inc". Also, make sure the preview text contains information relevant to the email contents and is interesting to the recipient.

The subject line is also important in improving the open rates. Personal subject lines seem to give better open rates. If your mailing solution allows for personalized email, use something like "Mark, here is your weekly stock market report" instead of "The weekly stock market report".

Finally, avoid spam triggers. Spam filters have learned that spam email often use certain words in the subject line, such as:

- $$$
- Buy
- Free

- Save
- Earn
- Credit
- Cheap

Search for "spam triggers" for a longer list.

Click-through rates

If all has gone well, you have both managed to deliver the email and got it opened. Now, the task is to make the email reader interact with you by responding to any of the offers in the email. An offer can be a link to further reading on your website or blog, or a call-to-action button that transfers the reader to a landing page with a web form offering a higher-value digital asset, such as an eBook, an infographics, or discount.

Just like with open rates, click-through rates can improve if the email is personalized (include the name in the subject line and once in the email body). Don't overdo the personalization, as it can get creepy if you try to be too personal.

The email copy should be short, clear, concise, and spacious with short paragraphs and bullet points to make it easy to scan. Don't make it look like a book that is daunting to read. Also include at least one relevant photo or image, and make sure the subject line, body, graphics, and calls-to-action are aligned to the same goal to provide a consistent offering.

From a marketing point of view, the most important thing in your marketing emails is the calls-to-action you include. Your email shall have one main call-to-action promoting the most important offer.

Make sure the call-to-action is prominent and obvious, and that it is located above the fold such that it is visible without scrolling down. It should stand out graphically (perhaps using signal colors), and have an actionable language like "Download now", "Register now", or "Get your eBook today".

It's a good idea to include multiple calls-to-action in the email, all driving traffic to the same landing page. You may, for example, have one big main graphical button and two or three hypertext links in the email body text pointing to the same page. That increases the likelihood your readers will click-through using one of them.

Don't forget that the main purpose of a marketing email is to make the reader engage and take the next step in the customer journey, pushing him or her towards the final goal of buying your product. Therefore, marketing emails should almost always contain an offer of some sort that entices the reader to engage further.

Spam flagging and unregister rates

If you want to keep sending emails to someone, you must ensure he or she is not displeased enough to spam-flag your email or unregister from your mailing list. In such a case, you have lost all future means of keeping in contact with this lead using email, and most likely you are not welcome to try.

What happened to cause a lead to spam-flag your email or unregister from your mailing list? There are several possible causes:

- The lead never registered to get any of your emails in the first place
- You send too many emails or too often
- You send emails with irrelevant content that does not interest the lead
- The lead had an interest in your products but no longer does
- The lead had a bad day, and you were unlucky

The best way to avoid spam flagging or unregistering is to:

- Only send email to leads who registered on your website or otherwise already have a relation with your company. Never buy email addresses or acquire them using other questionable means
- Avoid sending too many emails or too often

- Make sure the content is consistent with the subject line
- Make sure the content is of high quality
- Make sure the content interests this lead. Do not send emails that can reasonably be expected to be irrelevant to this lead

Even if you do things right, you will get unsubscribes. You are doing fine if your mailshot has less than 0.2% unsubscribes. If you have over 1%, your leads are not as happy to hear from you as they should be. Spam flagging should happen even less. Look into it if you are not within these limits.

Mailing solutions

When sending bulk emails (thousands, or even hundreds of thousands of emails), it is impractical to use your normal email client like Microsoft Outlook. You do not want to use your personal email address as the sender of mass emails either. Additionally, you should not use your normal company email server to send mailshots. This will harm your normal email correspondence should your mailshots reduce your sender score or even blacklist the email server altogether.

For automated emails, use a separate mailing service. There are many emailing service providers available, like MailChimp, Campaign Monitor, GetResponse, and AWeber. Search for "email newsletter service" or "marketing email provider" to find more. Many of them can host registration forms and manage your leads database. Some mass email service providers also offer reactive leads nurturing email workflows (drip email marketing).

An email service provider should track and present the open and click-through rates of your emails, list what leads have opened the email (or not), and show what links each lead has clicked. They often provide other types of interesting information too. An email service provider I used for a while showed the leads that opened the email on a graphical map in real-time, as it happened! It was fascinating to watch the world map and see how the email was being opened in different cities and countries at the same moment it occurred.

Another interesting email services supplier is Litmus. They don't send emails for you, but offer various other email related services in the areas of spam filter testing, email analytics, and email previews.

For a fully integrated leads nurturing experience, you may also want to look into a marketing automation system (which we'll discuss later).

Chapter summary

This chapter outlined best practices in sending emails, including proactive leads nurturing using mailshots, and reactive leads nurturing using drip email campaigns. The difficulty of making success with monthly newsletter emails was mentioned too.

Legal matters, as well as delivery rates, open rates, and click-through rates have been discussed, along with spam filter issues. Different solutions for sending emails were also presented.

The next chapter will provide additional details on search engines and advertisements.

Search engines, ads and more

No book on Internet marketing can ignore search engines like Google, Yahoo, or Bing. What are they and how do they work? Search engines crawl the Internet, analyze websites, and index their content.

Whenever someone searches for a keyword or phrase, the search engine looks in the index database to find the web pages it thinks are most relevant. These pages are presented in the search engine results pages (SERPs), with only ten links visible on the first page, ten more on the next page, and so on.

Getting into the first search engine results page is incredibly important, as few people bother to check page two or three, and even less for later pages. Clearly, the top one or two links get a lot more clicks than the ones further down on the first page. The position of a web page in the search results pages is called its rank. The better your web pages rank for a certain search keyword, the higher they will be listed in the search engine results pages, and the more traffic you will get.

Search engine optimization is about making your pages rank as high as possible in the search results pages (i.e. naturally or organically). Search engine advertisements, on the other hand, are a paid or sponsored way of getting your ads displayed on result pages. Search keyword analysis is about understanding what search keywords are popular and how tough the competition is to get visibility and organic traffic for those keywords.

There are also other types of advertisement concepts that can be used, including display advertisements and retargeting or remarketing. The following sections will outline the different options.

Search engine optimization

One of the hottest areas of Internet marketing for well over a decade has been Search Engine Optimization (SEO). The purpose of SEO is to modify your web pages such that they rank higher in the search results pages of Google and other search engines using certain keywords. This increases the likelihood the page will attract more organic (non-paid) traffic.

The rank of a web page is assessed by two things: its relevance and its authority. Relevance is determined by how well its content matches the search phrase, and authority is a measure of how important and trustworthy the search engine thinks your page and website are in other ways.

In terms of SEO, relevance has primarily been addressed by modifying or optimizing the page itself. This includes things like the occurrences of the search phrase and related search phrases or synonyms on the page, the amount of text and images, and readability. Authority can depend on the number of links to your web page there are on other websites, how old the domain name is, the number of visits to your website, its bounce rate and average visit duration, how fast your web server is, and how often your website is mentioned on social media.

I have read many books on SEO over the years and before starting to write this book, I expected this chapter would be the largest and most complicated by far. The problem is, there are so many SEO tricks to employ, and it is a moving target as Google and other search engines modify their search algorithms all the time. But before studying current SEO strategies, let's turn back and look into the history of search engine optimization.

History

In the early days, search engines didn't do much more than count the number of times a specific keyword existed on a web page, thus creating a relative rank between different web pages for a specific search phrase. This led some web designers to fake relevance by adding the keywords many times (keyword stuffing), sometimes in invisible ways like using white text on a white background. The search engines realized this, of course, and now punish websites using this trick. Not only does your ranking not improve, you make it a lot worse.

To serve their users with better content and fight numerous on-page SEO tricks, search engines started to measure the authority of web pages. For example, by counting the number of other websites linking to it. The thinking was that if many other (supposedly) independent websites refer to a page, it has to contain better content than a page with fewer inbound links.

What did black-hat SEO specialists do? They created a large number of fake websites with the sole purpose of adding pages with links back to the real web page whose authority they tried to improve. The search engines retaliated, of course, by considering the authority and quality of the linking websites before using them as references for good content, and punishing websites that seemed to be using link farms.

This has gone on for years, with SEO tricks being deployed and search engines blocking the attempts and punishing websites using them. In short, search engines like Google want their service to provide as good and useful search results as possible to their users, while website owners want their web pages to rank as high as possible. It is a constant battle.

Luckily, the search engines have become very good at detecting and punishing innovative SEO tricks, and deliver the pages with most relevant content. Therefore, it has become easier to do SEO these days. Unless you do online marketing as a full-time job, ignore all the hundreds of SEO advice that used to be recommended, and focus on writing good valuable content for your human readers instead. The search engines will notice in the end.

Well, almost. You should still be aware of a couple of things about relevance and authority.

Relevance

First, make sure to add new high-quality content regularly. An active website with weekly updates (think blog here!) will rank better than a website that has not been updated for years.

Second, search engines can only index text. A web page with mostly photos or other graphics is not good from a SEO point of view. Make sure each page has a reasonable amount of relevant text content if you want search engines to rank it well. The more, the better, as long as it is relevant to the topic.

Also notice that search engines nowadays consider the readability of your text. The readability of a text can be measured using the Flesch reading score. A score under 30 is best understood by university graduates, while a score in the range 60-70 is easily understood by 13-15 year olds. Try to keep your readability at 75 or above to keep search engines and your audience happy. You can test the readability of your web pages using this tool:
https://readability-score.com/

Do not practice keyword stuffing, but to increase the relevance, you need to add the most relevant search keywords to:

- The page title
- The page URL
- The page meta description
- The page heading
- A couple of times in the page body

The page title, URL, and meta description are visible in the Google search results as follows:

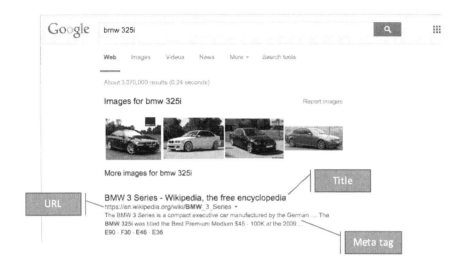

When it comes to the page URL, make sure it is search engine friendly. This means the page does not have an obscure URL like www.mysite.com/a9889?p=45, but rather something like www.mysite.com/learn_to_cook_sous_vide. If your content management system creates obscure URLs, install a plugin to make them friendly to search engines. Any modern content management system should have support for this.

Search engine optimization these days is not about trying to outsmart search engines, but to offer content of real value, thus helping them to offer your web pages to their users. However, you do need to analyze what search keywords you want to optimize the page for.

Try to optimize your pages for search keywords that are relevant to your offering, as you will otherwise get traffic from keywords that have little value to you. You also want to optimize your pages for keywords that have a lot of traffic, as it is meaningless to be in the top of the search result pages for search phrases that no one uses. You will not get a lot of useful traffic even though you rank as number one.

Finally, you don't want to compete for traffic using keywords that are difficult, for example because large global corporations with a lot higher website authority also compete for them. You are unlikely to rank higher than Adidas and Reebok for "sports shoes" no matter how you try.

75

When you decide what keywords to optimize a web page for, you need to balance the keyword relevance, search volume, and rank difficulty, and pick relevant search keywords that give you the best possible chance of getting a high rank and a lot of traffic. If the competition is too tough for short-tailed keywords (like "sports shoes"), try more specific long-tailed keywords (like "sports shoes for marathon running" or "long distance running sports shoes"), which are likely to have less competition.

If you can't get traffic for short-tailed keywords with too tough competition, at least you can take the traffic from the slightly less popular longer-tailed versions.

Authority

Try to build authority by getting as many good and relevant websites as possible to link back to your page. With high-quality content, you will get more inbound links over time, thus helping to improve your authority too. But remember, all websites are not equal. Getting links from highly popular quality websites gives you a better authority than links from obscure websites with no visitors.

Getting many inbound links organically may take time. There are strategies to add them more quickly, but beware, some approaches may be counterproductive. Just like email address lists, never buy links from link farms. Google will most likely notice and punish you. Also, link-swapping with other websites is likely to be detected by Google and may provide less value than other links. Links should be attained at a natural pace over time to be trustworthy in the eyes of the search engines.

You can create some initial links on your own by linking to your website from your company profile pages on YouTube, Facebook, LinkedIn, and other social media platforms. Include links to your website in every social media post you publish.

An effective approach is to use unprotected digital assets as link bait. Promote eBooks or other digital content for free, and it is likely other web pages will start to recommend your valuable document by linking to it from other web pages or blog posts.

Another link building trick is to distribute press releases using PR sites like **www.prweb.com** or **www.prnewswire.com** to promote your link bait if you have no other news to share. Press releases can spiral off and be published on a large number of media and blog sites, quickly creating many inbound links.

Constant change

The search engine algorithms are refined all the time. For example, in a recent major update to the search algorithm (known as Mobilegeddon), Google made a crackdown on websites not adapted for mobile users. If you want your pages to rank well, you now need to have a responsive website suitable for mobile users too (a responsive website auto-adapts its layout to fit devices with smaller screens).

You can expect SEO to continue to be a moving target. If you are interested in learning more about the Google search algorithm change history, check out this page: **https://moz.com/google-algorithm-change**.

To learn more on what factors affect your ranking on Google, you can read the "Search rankings 2015" report from Search Metrics or the MOZ "Search Engine Ranking Factors" survey:
http://www.searchmetrics.com/knowledge-base/ranking-factors/
https://moz.com/search-ranking-factors

MOZ is a well-respected authority in the SEO industry and offers a lot of useful content. For example, their blog (**https://moz.com/blog**) provides interesting reading if you want to dive deeper into this subject.

You may also find Alexa of interest. They provide competitor intelligence and benchmarking services: **http://www.alexa.com**.

Search engine advertisement

Search engine optimization is all about getting more traffic for free. Search engine advertisement, on the other hand, is a paid alternative for getting traffic from search engines. With search engine advertisement, you can get a lot of relevant traffic immediately, which might be a good alternative to SEO, which takes time (often months) to become effective. The downside, of course, is it costs money.

For example, Google has AdWords, which is their search engine advertisement offering to businesses. With Google AdWords, you can pay to get a small, text only advert shown above, below, or to the right of the search result pages. Your advert only shows when someone searches for the specific keywords you have connected to your advert. You can define in detail when the advert will be published (for example, limit its visibility by country or city, by language, or by time-of-day).

You typically define a long list of similar keywords, all related to your offering, and show one or more adverts whenever any of those keywords are used in a search. You pay per click, not per ad impression. The price for the advert (cost per click, CPC) goes up and down all the time depending on the competition for advertisement space for the same keywords. You can define a quota for your daily spending, meaning you can control your budget.

There are many parameters to set in Google AdWords related to bidding strategies, and I recommend you study how the platform works before starting to spend money on it.

Search keyword analysis

Before writing web pages or blog articles, or even digital assets like eBooks or whitepapers, you can research how popular different topics are on the Internet. You can do this using search keyword analysis. This helps you write content that targets what most readers are interested in, and it helps you avoid fighting against tough competition in organic search results or paid search engine advertisements.

In short, you want to create content that covers the topics and keywords most people seem to be interested in. However, more web pages may write about topics containing one search keyword than another. This makes it harder or easier to succeed in achieving a good ranking (at the top) of the search engine results pages.

In a search keyword analysis tool, you typically enter all combinations of relevant search phrases to find out which ones are most likely to give the best ROI (most reader interest with least competition). You will likely get 100 or more combinations of keyword phrases in your list, which you submit to the tool for analysis.

For example, a Manhattan-based web shop selling wine may want to capture traffic for these keywords:

- Red wine
- White wine
- French wines
- Spanish wines
- Sparkling wines
- Wine with cheese
- Wine for salmon
- Wine tasting glasses
- Wine tasting equipment
- Wine cooler
- Manhattan wine tasting
- Manhattan wine training
- …

To successfully get organic traffic from search engines, people will have to find you in the search results pages of Google or other search engines. Ideally, your pages should be in the top three positions on the first page. If you are not in any of the first two or three pages, almost no one will find you.

This makes it rather hopeless if you are in a common industry. Trying to rank well for general terms like "red wine" may be hard, for example. The trick here is to use longer-tailed keywords instead. By targeting more specific keyword combinations, you have a higher chance of a better ranking.

For example, a short-tailed keyword may be "sports cars". You may not get your pages to rank at the top of search engine result pages for this. But a long-tailed version may well work, like "Italian sports cars" or "Ferrari sports cars in California".

Many tools exist to do search keyword research. They can usually provide auto-generated suggestions for new search phrase combinations based on your initial keywords. Additionally, they can provide statistical data on how popular various search keywords are (what traffic volumes they have) and their competition (how difficult it is to rank well for them).

Search for "search keyword analysis tool" to find a list of tools to choose from, or try the Google AdWords keyword planning tool (it is free but requires registration—find it under the "Tools" menu): **https://adwords.google.com/KeywordPlanner**

For more keyword ideas, you may want to try Ubersuggest. This generates a list of related keywords based on your initial keyword: **http://ubersuggest.org**

The Moz Keyword Difficulty and SERP Analysis Tool can help you analyze how tough the competition is for your desired keywords: **https://moz.com/tools/keyword-difficulty**

Display advertisement

Display advertisement (sometimes referred to as banner ads) is the name of an ad that promotes your offering on another website. Usually, an ad is a paid graphical advertisement, and by clicking on it, a user is transferred to your website or one of your landing pages. You usually pay per click (PPC), but ads can also be paid per ad impression, or using a flat fee per week or month.

You can pay for an ad on the website of a magazine or some other well-known portal relevant to your business. If you don't know any specific website you want to advertise on, you can use an advertisement network. Advertisement networks act as brokers between website owners selling advertisement space and advertisement buyers who want to place an ad on relevant Internet sites.

There are many display advertisement networks that offer to display your ads on various websites, and the Google Ads Display Network (GDN) can be a good starting point if you are interested in this. The sheer number of websites participating in their network makes it easier to find sites with the right profile.

Designing a display advertisement or banner ad is much like designing an advertisement for print media, but it may contain animations (in GIF or PNG format). They usually contain a call-to-action text that entices the viewer to click on it, thus driving traffic to your website or landing page. Ads can also be in video format.

In addition to paid ads using display advertisement networks, you can also ask other website owners for free advertisements in return for something else they may want. For example, propose having their adverts displayed on your website for free in return.

Retargeting and remarketing

Retargeting (sometimes also called remarketing) is a relatively new concept, where your advertisements can chase your previous website visitors around the Internet when they visit completely unrelated websites. In other words, visitors to your website continue to see your ads on other websites after they have left your site.

In effect, retargeting provides Internet advertisements based on previous browsing history across different websites. Retargeting is implemented using a tracking cookie, enabling an advertisement broker to know if a visitor to some other website has previously visited yours. If so, your advertisement will be displayed on the other unrelated website.

Google, for example, offers retargeting advertisement services, but they call it remarketing. Using static remarketing, your ad can be shown to people who previously visited your site, and have moved on to other ones. Given the size of the Google advertisement network, this is likely to happen rather often.

With dynamic remarketing, different advertisement designs (for example promoting different product models) can be shown depending on what pages a visitor has viewed on your website. If a certain visitor viewed your laptop section, for example, they will see your laptop ads when they visit other websites. If the visitor on the other hand viewed your printer section, they will see your printer ads on other websites.

Using retargeting your ads will follow previous website visitors around the Internet, thus reminding them of their previous visit to your website and your offerings. But be a bit careful, some may feel retargeting haunts them if done too aggressively.

What happens if the visitor purchases your product? In this case, you don't want to continue paying for retargeting advertisements. You also don't want to upset the new customer by haunting him or her with continued retargeting advertisements that chase them around the Internet.

The trick is to use what is called a burn pixel. As soon as your website has detected this visitor is now a customer, a JavaScript code snippet (the burn pixel) placed in your post-transaction logic will un-tag the user from further retargeting advertisements.

Chapter summary

This chapter explained what search engines are and how they work, along with strategies for getting more organic traffic using search engine optimization (SEO).

Search engine marketing, search keyword analysis, and display advertisement was outlined too, along with information on retargeting and remarketing ads that follow your website visitors around the Internet.

The next chapter will provide information on social media marketing, including Facebook, Twitter, LinkedIn, YouTube, and SlideShare.

Social media and content sharing platforms

No one has ignored the strong expansion of social media sites like Facebook, LinkedIn, or Twitter, but how can these channels be used for marketing? Like blog articles, they can help promote your brand name, increase your thought leadership level, and drive traffic to your blog or website. Most of them offer more or less the same thing: a flow of posts, each containing a title, a photo, and perhaps a couple of paragraphs of additional text. That helps, as the same content can be pushed out to the different social media channels with little modification.

Since it takes time to write a lot of content, my advice is to simply push out shortened versions of your blog articles on Facebook, Twitter, and LinkedIn. That way you get a reasonable exposure to the benefits of these marketing channels, at little effort on top of writing your blog articles in the first place. Some marketing automation systems and social media management tools can even do this automatically.

In addition to these well-known social media sites, there are also content publishing platforms that act like social media sites to some extent. These include YouTube for video sharing and SlideShare for publishing presentations.

Facebook

Facebook is the number one social media by far, with its 1.5 billion or so monthly users, and it can be considered the biggest meeting place in the world. Naturally, Facebook can be a great place for marketing, though it is better suited for marketing towards consumers rather than to businesses. A local coffee shop or a company selling ecological child food will likely be more successful using Facebook marketing than a company selling ball bearing lubricants for industrial use.

The first thing you ought to do before you start a Facebook page for your business is to spend some time visiting the pages of other companies. In particular, study those of your competitors, those of related businesses in your industry, or any other company you admire. Like the blog, you should try to write a Facebook post a couple or several times a week.

In addition to using Facebook for organic marketing using posts people may read, like, and share, you may want to consider paid advertisement on Facebook. There are different ad types to consider:

- Send people to your website
- Increase conversions on your website
- Boost your posts
- Promote your page
- Get installs of your app
- Increase engagement in your app
- Reach people near your business
- Raise attendance at your event
- Get people to claim your offer
- Get video views

Facebook adverts can be targeted by criteria such as location, age, sex, relationship status, education, and more. You can also target Facebook ads based on interest or behavior.

You can also upload your leads database to Facebook. If one of the email addresses in your database is connected to a Facebook account, then you can target ads only to those Facebook members who are already in your leads database.

Twitter

Twitter is the fastest moving of the social media channels and has approximately 300 million users, and so is a lot smaller than Facebook. Twitter is like Facebook or your blog in that you can post ("tweet") messages and a photo. Unlike the blog or Facebook, a tweet can only be 140 characters long. Not much for a marketing message that needs to contain a link to your website!

Luckily, there are some tricks. For example, if you want to promote your new blog article by sending a tweet with a link to it, you can shorten the blog article title to something with the same meaning. You want all your tweets to contain a link to your website or blog, or else the purpose as a traffic generator is lost. But with the 140-character limit, how would you fit long URLs linking to your blog posts or web pages? The trick here is to use a URL shortener.

A URL shortener is an Internet service that takes your long URL link and creates a working copy of it with a much shorter length. There are several free services offering this. The most well-known is probably Bit.ly. By pasting a long URL into the Bit.ly website, you will get a completely different and much shorter URL back. The example below shows a link before and after Bit.ly URL shortening:

http://www.unemyr.com/marketing/how-self-published-authors-can-sell-more-non-fiction-books-internet-marketing-in-practice/

http://bit.ly/1M0eutK

To summarize, Bit.ly and similar sites can shorten long URLs so they are easier to use in your social media outreach. Use the shortened and obscure version if you are squeezed for space, as is the case with tweets.

You can also buy paid advertisements on Twitter, either to promote a tweet or promote your account to get more followers. With a promoted tweet, you pay to get a tweet displayed in people's feeds. With a promoted account, you pay to get more followers. Twitter enables targeting by some demographic parameters, as well as keywords. For example, you may target Twitter members who have posted or interacted with tweets containing a certain text.

LinkedIn

LinkedIn is primarily a social media channel for professionals, with approximately 350 million monthly users. Like Facebook, companies can have their profile page on LinkedIn too, but a LinkedIn company page can also have a separate section (a "tab") for product information.

A LinkedIn company page has a home page with company details, a photo, and news flow. There is a "Page insights" tab with statistics on page views and visits, and other insights tabs providing more detailed statistics.

LinkedIn visitors are usually more career oriented than those on Facebook and Twitter, and your profile page, content, and news flow should be more formal to match that. LinkedIn Ads is a paid advertisement solution on LinkedIn.

YouTube

While not a social media channel as such, YouTube is a tremendously successful platform for video sharing owned by Google. YouTube has over one billion visits every month and is the right place if you want your videos published to the general public. Users can search for keywords and YouTube will present a list of available videos relevant to that search phrase.

Videos published on YouTube are publicly available and do not generate any leads because they are not gated. But there is nothing that stops you from publishing a video on YouTube (for brand building, thought leadership, and traffic generation purposes) and the same video on your website with landing page protection (for leads generation). Visitors to YouTube or your website are unlikely to notice the same video is available elsewhere with different access protection.

Videos can make great marketing assets. For example, videos of educational value can include interviews, training videos, recorded webinars, or product demo videos. A video can record you or someone else talking in front of a webcam (or a smartphone these days), or it can show a narrated PowerPoint presentation or a recorded product demo.

If you want to record the computer screen, use screen recording software like Camtasia or Cam Studio. For video editing, the free Apple iMovie or Microsoft Windows Movie Maker is fine in many cases.

When recording the video, make sure there are no disturbing background sounds (such as trains passing by), and if you record the computer screen, embarrassing popup notifications should be disabled. Make sure the videos include a call-to-action driving traffic to your website. In particular, do not end the movie with a black frame. Instead, add a call-to-action.

If you produce multiple videos, you can create a YouTube channel (it is like a playlist) that helps your viewers to find your other videos. If visitors get interested in the videos you publish, they can register with YouTube to get a notification email when you release additional videos. You can also tag your movies with certain keywords, helping people to find your movie should they search for those topics.

A company that leverages YouTube exceptionally well is Molecule-R, a Canadian company selling equipment and food additives for Molecular Gastronomy (a modern and advanced type of cooking). Molecule-R has published a large number of exceptional video tutorials on how to cook using their products. Search for "Molecule-R" on YouTube to see what I mean. No doubt their beautiful cooking videos on YouTube help generate a lot of sales for them.

Paid YouTube ads are short videos that play before other videos start. They can also be promoted in video search results or beside other videos. You can define which search keywords or demography of visitors should trigger your video ad.

SlideShare

SlideShare is similar to YouTube in that it is primarily a content sharing platform. As the name suggests, it is designed for sharing presentations. SlideShare is owned by LinkedIn, and claims to be one of the top 100 most visited websites in the world, with 70 million visitors every month.

You can upload presentations and other documents for public sharing. Supported file formats are PDF, Microsoft Word and PowerPoint files, and the OpenOffice equivalents. Once uploaded, the documents become searchable and browse-able. You can embed SlideShare hosted presentations into your web pages and blog articles, thus making those documents browse-able right on your own website.

Add clickable calls-to-action (hyperlinks) to your presentations to drive traffic to your website, blog articles, or landing pages. If you have no other ideas for calls-to-action, drive traffic to a landing page offering the reader a download of the presentation as a high-resolution PDF (in this case, switch off the default SlideShare behavior of offering unguarded PDF downloads).

SlideShare can be used for leads generation, as it can show custom designed leads capture forms. You can define where and how the registration forms should appear in your content.

Similar to traditional social media sites, SlideShare allows viewers to "like" presentations and "follow" content creators (i.e. you). You can see who shares your content, where visitors come from, and what search terms brought them to your presentation.

Some marketing automation systems integrate with SlideShare, such that captured leads are automatically transferred into the leads database of the marketing automation system.

Social media management

Managing and monitoring many social media channels concurrently may be impractical and time consuming. Hootsuite is a tool you can use to publish on many social media platforms simultaneously, and let you engage with people across all your social media accounts through a single dashboard. Hootsuite also includes social media monitoring and analysis.

Marketing automation systems often include social media management features too.

Chapter summary

This chapter focused on how to use social media marketing for organic traffic generation and paid ads, including Facebook, Twitter, LinkedIn, YouTube, and SlideShare.

The next chapter will reveal what marketing automation systems are, and what they can do for you.

Marketing automation systems

So far, we have covered how to attract visitors using your website and blog, and how to promote them using email, social media, search engines, or paid advertising. We have also covered how to convert visitors to leads and nurture them. Many of these things can be done manually or using separate tools. The real power, however, comes when you bring them together into a fully integrated and automated system. This is called marketing automation, and the software products doing this are called marketing automation systems.

Let's face it: Creating landing pages with registration forms, storing contact information into a leads database, sending delivery emails, and displaying a thank you page is not easy to set up manually. Especially not if you want to do something useful with the newly captured lead, such as sending them new email offers automatically a few days apart using a leads nurturing workflow. And this is not something you do once. Every blog article and web page should promote a landing-page-guarded digital asset if you want them to generate leads, and so you need to make new call-to-action buttons, landing pages, and nurturing workflows all the time.

If you can afford it, a good marketing automation system is your online marketing dream come true. These systems provide so many capabilities you would not have been able to build yourself in any other way. They are accessible to anyone, as they require only basic IT knowledge. A marketing automation system can help you get a deep understanding of the behavior and interest of your visitors and leads by detecting and analyzing their digital body language, and then automatically personalize your marketing message to each individual visitor.

The top three systems (other vendors may argue here) are HubSpot, SalesForce Pardot, and Marketo. To find more options, search for "marketing automation systems," or if you are a small company, try "free marketing automation systems". Most of these systems charge monthly, with different prices dependent on the number of leads in the database or number of emails being sent from the system. Some systems are also entirely free unless you break a leads or email count threshold, and so they could work well for small companies with low lead and email volumes.

Marketing automation systems do many things. Your mileage will vary depending on what product you chose, but the best ones can handle things like:

- Search keyword analysis. This help you find what search engine keywords are used most and how hard it is to get a good ranking for them. Use this feature to find out what blog articles would give the best effect, and what digital assets are most sought after.

- Visitor and leads tracking. With the help of tracking cookies on your website and blog, all online visitor activities are recorded and tracked for later use, even before you know who the visitors are. For example, you can see that a visitor often comes back to the swim gear section of your website, but never visits the yoga clothes section. A marketing automation system can use this knowledge in ingenious ways.

- Call-to-action generators. Quickly create call-to-action buttons that promote your offers and drive traffic to your landing pages. The best marketing automation systems even support smart call-to-action buttons, where the design and behavior changes dynamically dependent on what the visitor has been doing on the website in the past.

- Landing page and thank you page editor. Quickly add new landing pages with registration forms. In the same manner, easily create thank you pages that are displayed automatically once the landing page form is submitted. The system can typically send an email to the lead automatically to deliver the requested digital asset or just to thank him or her for their interest in your offerings.

- Registration form editor. The form editor lets you effortlessly design what fields a form should have. The best marketing automation systems even support smart fields, which removes the need for leads to enter the same information several times if they register in multiple landing pages. Smart forms remember what question fields a lead has already filled in and replace those questions with other queued questions instead. Why? To get more information on the lead over time, without putting him or her off by asking too many questions at a time.

- Leads database. Since a registration form collects information about leads, this information must be stored somewhere. This is the job of the leads database. With a marketing automation system, you get this as an integrated part of the system, including capabilities to filter the full list into segmented lists of leads fulfilling certain criteria. The system must allow you to define custom data fields that relate to your particular needs, and it should track the complete activity history of any lead automatically.

- Workflow logic. Worthy marketing automation systems let you define flowcharts of custom-defined logic that starts automatically when something happens. Workflows can be triggered when a registration form is submitted, an email has been opened, a web page was visited, or other events happen. Workflows perform actions such as sending emails, updating information in the leads database, and so on.

- Leads scoring. Leads scoring is about designing a formula for assessing how sales-ready an individual lead is, based on his or her previous online activity history. If he or she has triggered enough traps, the lead is considered valuable enough for a sales representative to spend time on. Marketing automation systems allow you to design the leads-scoring algorithm, and they run the monitoring for you automatically.

- CRM integration. Many marketing automation systems have integration bridges with popular customer relationship management systems, such that leads and their latest status can automatically be synchronized bi-directionally between the two systems.

- VMP integration. Video Marketing Platforms like Wistia and VidYard can integrate with many marketing automation systems. Leads captured by gated videos are transferred to the marketing automation system. In addition to the contact information, detailed video-viewing behaviors of each lead can be synchronized as well. This enables the marketing automation system to use video viewing patterns in workflows, leads scoring, segmentation, or other decision logic.

- Blog engine. A marketing automation system can also host your blog, such that you do not need to redo your existing website. If the marketing automation system hosts the blog, it automatically lists a summary of the latest ten or so posts on the blog front-page, include a commenting system, and group articles by topic or author. It also handles notification emails to readers who have signed up for an instant, daily, weekly, or monthly blog round-up notification email.

- Smart content. Marketing automation systems can personalize the content of a web page or an email based on information the system has on a particular lead. Content can change automatically for a specific visitor depending on the country of the lead, if the person has submitted a specific registration form, opened an email, or some other decision criteria from the leads database.

- Emails. A marketing automation system sends delivery, nurturing, or notification emails upon certain events. This is the kind of transactional emails that are sent one-by-one as a result of an individual event being triggered. Marketing automation systems also include the capability for mailshots, which are typically used for newsletter emails, campaign outreach, or the like. Email content can often be personalized, such that data like lead name, city, or company name are pasted into certain positions in the email. Some marketing automation systems even allow emails to contain smart content.

- Campaigns. If you want to group certain things for statistical analysis and reporting (this is intentionally vague), you can use campaigns as the grouping and metering device. Tag various objects like certain calls-to-action, landing pages, and digital assets as belonging to a campaign, and then monitor the marketing performance of all the objects working together in the campaign.

- Social media integration. Marketing automation systems can integrate with your social media accounts, such as Facebook, LinkedIn, and Twitter. You can then use the system to push out messages automatically to all social media channels. Marketing automation systems typically include features for monitoring of the activities of your social media channels, as well as other types of reporting.

- Website integration. Get HTML/JavaScript code snippets from the marketing automation system and paste them into your website to integrate the functionality. One example is to add a smart call-to-action button or a registration form to a web page. Some marketing automation systems are full content management systems in their own right, enabling you to run your regular company website using the marketing automation platform as your hosting solution as well.

- Media manager. Upload digital assets and other files to the online media library of the marketing automation system, and easily use them on web pages, blog articles, and landing or thank you pages.

- Analytics and reporting. Since the marketing automation system is super-integrated, it knows everything about the marketing performance of web pages, blog articles, emails, landing page form submissions, social media activity, lead activities, and how the leads database evolves. This enables it to provide a wide variety of highly useful statistics on how pieces of your online marketing system perform, including cross-tabulated data on different types of data points.

In the following sections, I will go into some more detail about the capabilities of marketing automation systems.

Search keyword analysis tool

A marketing automation system may have an integrated keyword search analysis tool. If not, use a standalone tool as outlined in an earlier chapter. Use the search keyword analysis functionality to find what keywords most people are searching for, and how difficult it is to compete for good ranking on them. This helps understand which blog articles or documents can have the best marketing effect.

Visitor and leads tracking

One of the most useful, and some would argue scary, things are the possibility to track what a particular website visitor has been doing on a website. From a marketing point of view, it enables websites to track what web pages a visitor has seen, how many times, and when.

Technically, this tracking is done using cookies. A cookie is a small piece of information a website can store on the visitor's computer. The same website can read back that data the next time the visitor returns. This gives websites the possibility to store information from earlier visits for use later.

For you, it means that once an anonymous visitor has registered on a landing page and become an identified lead, you can start to record their activities. This information is then stored in a database inside the marketing automation system, and you can check exactly what every lead has been doing on your website. To be useful, there needs to be a reporting panel of some sort as well.

For example, you can see that one lead comes back several times a day, while another one only comes back once or twice a month. Guess which one is most likely to buy something from you? You can also see that a lead visits your web pages on cocktail equipment all the time but never reads your web pages on cooking equipment.

Which of your two mailshot versions is most likely to trigger a sale, the cocktail equipment newsletter or the cooking equipment newsletter? What type of discount offer would be most efficient with this lead? A 20% discount on cocktail or cooking equipment?

The implementation of visitor tracking on a website is relatively straightforward. The website creates a unique visitor ID number connected to that specific lead, and writes this number into a cookie on the visitor's computer. Whenever the same visitor comes back to the website, the web pages contain a small HTML/JavaScript code snippet that tries to read back that visitor ID number from the cookie.

If the cookie exists on the computer, this visitor has been to the website before, and he or she is already stored in the database. It is then possible to cross reference the visitor ID number from the cookie with the database to work out who this visitor is, and to update the usage statistics in the database. Over time, as visitors browse your website pages, you will get an excellent overview of how interested different leads are in your products, and which products too! If the cookie doesn't exist, it is not possible to connect the visit to any particular person or previous visit.

There are two cases in which the above logic does not work. Since cookies have been a bit of a sensitive subject for privacy reasons, web browsers allow users to disable cookies altogether. They also allow web browser users to remove the cookie data from the computer. In both cases, there will be no cookies storing information from earlier visits, and visitor tracking using cookies will not work. Most people still have cookies enabled, though. There are also regulations on cookie use in many countries these days, enforcing opt-in before a website may use cookies. This is why you increasingly see "I approve" buttons for cookie use.

Having the capability to get statistics on how often leads visit your website, and what pages they read, is very useful for marketing purposes, not to mention for the ability to update yourself on a lead's interests before you make a sales call to him or her. When you call them, you can speak enthusiastically about the new exotic plants you recently imported from Asia (if website visitor statistics shows this is their primary interest), and tune down on roses and tulips altogether.

And there's more. Creating a cookie with a unique visitor ID number also works for website visitors who have not yet converted into a lead by entering their contact information in a registration form. Therefore, you can track the website usage of anonymous visitors too.

But what use would you possibly have for behavior statistics for people if you do not know who they are? You can't email them offers, and you can't give them a sales call either. After all, how would you use the information that a particular anonymous visitor has come back to a specific web page 25 times while another one only two times? Using smart content, you can adapt a web page based on what pages they have most frequently visited before, even if you don't know who they are. If a lead is mostly on your tropical plants section, make sure that for him or her, offers on other web pages focus more on that topic too.

Read the following carefully and think about what this means! The trick is to combine the historical usage data from anonymous visitors with their identity once they convert in a registration form and become an identified lead. Just like leads that have provided their contact information on a landing page, anonymous visitors also get a unique visitor ID number cookie, which over time helps collect information about what web pages they have visited. After a long time of using your website anonymously, perhaps for months, they finally convert into a lead by registering on a landing page.

Their unique visitor ID number does not change when they convert— they are still the same Internet user browsing from the same computer containing the same visitor ID number tracking cookie. So, with their contact information now at hand, it becomes possible to backtrack everything they have done anonymously on the website for months or years! This enables you to know what their interest level is, and what topics interest them before you make that sales call.

You will find you know way more about them than they can ever anticipate, which gives you the upper hand. Even if they converted from an anonymous visitor to an identified lead today, you could mine the database and clearly see their interest seems to be marathon running and not playing football. At least according to, say, six months worth of browsing history. Even if you don't use this data in manual processes, automated workflows can and do benefit this way.

Call-to-action generators and smart CTAs

Marketing automation systems can include call-to-action generators that make it easy to create clickable buttons. The design phase is usually easy. You either create the CTA as a text button, in which case the button style can be configured using CSS, or you upload a bitmap image designed in some graphics software. The call-to-action generator additionally allows you to define the destination URL of the landing page.

If your marketing automation system includes features to host your website or blog, it may include an "insert CTA" command that makes it easy to use the call-to-action button on those pages. If your website or blog is hosted by an external system, the marketing automation system can include an "embed CTA" command. This generates a small piece of HTML/JavaScript code that you can insert into the HTML code of the web page or blog article of the externally hosted system to add the button.

Why all these steps for something as simple as creating a bitmap image button and link to a landing page? Why not just insert an image into the web page or blog article, and add a hyperlink to it? In other words, why integrate a call-to-action generator in a marketing automation system in the first place?

The main point here is not to use it as a convenience function to create the buttons more quickly. However, it is useful that once the call-to-action is defined as an object in the marketing automation software, the system can track its usage statistics, and hence its marketing performance. The marketing automation system will provide you with detailed information on how often website visitors actually click on the call-to-action button to get to the landing page. This is usually measured in percent of total page views (the click-through rate).

Why is this important? First, you can change the call-to-action design to see if it improves or reduces the click-through rate (i.e. its marketing performance). Even small changes to color, layout, or title may affect the click-through rate. For example, a boring gray button with the text "Read the eBook on fishing" may perform less well than a more graphical version in a bright green signal color with the title "Read our FREE eBook on Fishing now!" Especially if it includes an image of a fish or two.

This manual performance testing can be taken one step further with a marketing automation system. Using A/B testing, you can define two alternate implementations of the call-to-action, and the marketing automation system can then randomly show both versions to different visitors during the testing period and measure how they each perform.

After a sufficient time (this depends on the amount of web traffic you have, but once the statistical data is large enough for a conclusive measurement), remove the least performing version and keep the better one. In fact, the marketing automation system may do this for you automatically. You can keep doing this with a second and third A/B testing if you like, continuing to challenge the best performer with new versions and always taking the next winner as your new baseline.

But there is more, and I find this part particularly interesting. While A/B testing is useful, the most compelling reason to use the marketing automation system to do the CTAs is smart calls-to-action. With a smart call-to-action, the CTA button can change its look and behavior on-the-fly for different visitors, based on certain knowledge the system may have about them. Maybe the system knows what city or country this visitor lives in, or it may know he or she visits the website section on red wine more often than that on white wine. It may know he or she already downloaded an eBook. What can you do with all this?

Let's continue with an example of a wine webshop. Assume you have a call-to-action button on your home page offering an eBook on wine tasting. This serves as an excellent default digital asset to offer new visitors, especially before you know anything about them.

But what happens after this visitor has already registered to read that eBook? The call-to-action offering that digital asset serves no purpose anymore, as he or she has already consumed this offer. The CTA could now be more effective with another offer, promoting something else, like an online wine tasting webinar or a wine tasting video tutorial.

Maybe the usage statistics of this visitor shows they are interested in Spanish wines from the Rioja region. Perhaps the default CTA offering an eBook on wine tasting is not the best one for this person. It would probably be more effective to have a CTA offering something related to Spanish Rioja wines, perhaps an eBook called "Learn more about the Rioja wine region".

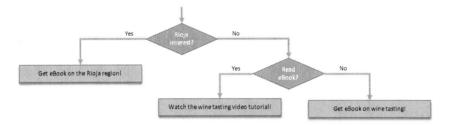

Could this work? It sounds like magic for a marketer, but the marketing automation system contains website visitor tracking for anonymous visitors as well as converted leads with known contact information. It also includes a leads database where additional information on the lead may be recorded. Thus, it is possible to define logic in the marketing automation system that decides which offer to use in a CTA dependent on various visitor criteria.

And so, for a smart CTA for the wine webshop home page, you can display the default wine tasting eBook offer when you don't yet know enough about the visitor. If they have already consumed the default eBook offer, the smart CTA changes automatically to show the offer for a wine tasting video tutorial instead, hopefully driving this visitor closer to a sale. On the other hand, if website usage statistics show this visitor has frequented the Rioja section of Spanish wines more than anywhere else on the website, the smart CTA shows the offer "Learn more about the Rioja wine region".

This is really clever and helps to show a razor-sharp focus that fits each website visitor individually and perfectly. Of course, you cannot make CTAs, landing pages, and digital offers like eBooks or video tutorials for each specific individual's needs down to the smallest detail. Even just offering the three or four most obvious ones can make a big difference as your offers match the visitor's needs and interests more closely—Or so he or she perceives it, at least.

In my opinion, smart CTAs are among the most important features of a good marketing automation system.

Landing page and thank you page editor

Landing pages have a focused purpose: to convert anonymous visitors into leads with known contact information, or to collect more data on an existing lead. Once the landing page form has been submitted, you show a thank you page with more offers trying to keep the visitor engaging a bit longer.

What can marketing automation systems do to help here? First, they typically contain a WYSIWYG (what you see is what you get) HTML editor to enable you to easily design the landing page with its titles, body text, and graphics. A marketing automation system also allows you to place a registration form on the landing page.

Second, a marketing automation system hosts the landing and thank you pages for you, providing an easy solution to quickly get them up and running outside of your normal website. They also handle integration between the registration forms and the leads database, which is quite convenient, as it is not easy for novice non-techie website owners to build this.

The details of the registration form design are important, and are covered in their own section below. For the purpose of the landing page, for the time being just accept that you can easily insert a registration form asking for contact details.

Like CTAs, good marketing automation systems let you perform A/B testing of landing pages to measure which variations perform best. A/B testing of landing pages is a bit more difficult, as they contain more parameters than a call-to-action button. For example, does an Excel formula template, webinar training, or an eBook generate the most submissions? What title, body text, or image makes more visitors submit the form? What registration form frightens visitors the least, and what font or color scheme works best?

Once the visitor has finally submitted the landing page form, they have closed their part of the deal. You got the contact details and perhaps answers to some additional questions too. Now it is your turn to deliver on your promise to provide the digital asset you offered.

As mentioned earlier, this can be done using two different methods, either by immediately sending a delivery e-mail with the digital asset or with instructions on how to download it, or by publishing it directly on the thank you page for immediate download.

In either case, the thank you page should be displayed automatically as soon as the landing page form is submitted. This should be handled by your marketing automation system, as should the sending of the delivery email if you prefer that route.

Registration form editor

Creating registration forms without a marketing automation system or something similar is not very easy. It involves creating the form with question fields, implementing the logic of the Submit button, and making sure the form data is stored in a leads database somewhere for later use. It also involves adding field validation to prevent illegal data from being accepted by the form. Common types of input validation include checking for non-existing countries, invalid numbers, or erroneously constructed dates, phone numbers, and email addresses.

Implementing the registration form and its underlying logic is a barrier if you have to resort to HTML and JavaScript coding. It might be easier if you use registration form plug-ins in content management systems like WordPress or Joomla, or the services of a mailing system supplier. But a marketing automation system makes things easy for you. You can design the form by adding the fields you want, sometimes using a drag and drop designer. The system will host the form for you, including field validation and recording the submitted data into the leads database.

It is important that you can add your own custom data fields to the leads database, also enabling the registration forms to capture this information. All companies need to store basic leads information like name, company, and address, but you probably want to store information specific to your business or industry too. The custom data fields you add to the leads database should be possible to add to the registration forms.

Marketing automation systems have provided us with the means to do some additional wizardry not possible before. Are there any tricks up their sleeve here too? In fact, yes. Like smart call-to-action buttons that can change the look and behavior based on what the system knows about the visitor, there are also smart forms.

As I mentioned earlier, there is a struggle between you as a marketer wanting to ask more questions in the form, and the visitor who refuses to fill-in and submit the form if it asks too many or too personal questions. What can a marketing automation system do to help? Smart forms are a clever solution.

Smart forms allow us to ask more questions without asking more questions. At one time, that is. A smart form remembers which form fields a lead has filled out previously in other registration forms, and avoids asking the same questions to the same lead again (the magic of leads tracking comes into play here). Instead, other new questions are shifted in to replace the fields that have already been answered.

Some fields may have to be answered repeatedly, like the email address. There would otherwise not be any possibility for the visitor to correct a mistyped email address. But for all fields that are not strictly mandatory to ask each time, questions already answered are shifted out, and new ones are added to replace them.

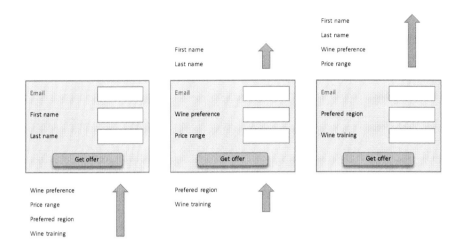

That way you can learn more about your leads over time, provided they continue to submit forms to consume additional digital assets that you promote to them. This is progressive profiling.

The first time a lead registers a form, he or she may have to answer these questions:

- Email
- First name
- Last name

The next time the same lead submits a different form to get access to another digital asset, he or she may get these form questions instead:

- Email
- Wine preference? (red, white or sparkling)
- What price range is acceptable for a bottle of wine? (10 USD, 15 USD, 20USD or more)

Only the email field is visible again, for reasons outlined above. The remaining two fields now ask different questions, thus collecting additional information about this lead. Later, the same lead submits one more form, and now the smart form again changes the set questions:

- Email
- What wine region do you prefer? (USA, Spain, France, South Africa)
- Are you interested in a wine tasting training course?

Using smart forms, you can ask many questions that over time provide you with a lot more information. If you craft your registration form questions carefully, you will get real insights into the interests of leads, helping you to send better focused and targeted marketing information and offers. This makes you appear more relevant to them, and you don't put them off by asking too many questions at a time.

The leads database

To make any use of the leads you capture in registration forms, you need to store them in a leads database for later use. This database is at the heart of the marketing automation system, and many of the system's capabilities interact with it. For example:

- Registration forms add information to the database
- Emails are sent to leads in the database
- Visitor tracking records what web pages and blog articles a lead has visited, what emails have been opened, and what registration forms have been submitted
- Subsets of leads can be defined using filtering or segmentation criteria to create smaller mailing lists for more specific mailshots
- Smart call-to-action buttons, smart content, and smart forms adapt their behavior for different visitors based on information from the database
- Nurturing workflow logic query the leads database to decide what follow-up emails should be sent automatically at various times

- Leads scoring algorithms query the database

All leads databases have data fields common to any company, such as name, email address, company, and the like. The leads database should also contain the activity history of each lead. This includes information on what registration forms have been filled in, what emails have been opened, and what web pages or blog articles have been visited. This type of information should be created and maintained automatically by the marketing automation system. To be truly useful, the leads database must also be configurable, allowing you to define custom data fields specific to your business or industry.

For example, if you are selling machinery for sign manufacturing, you may want to store information like:

- Does this lead use engraving, laser marking, or vinyl cutters to make the signs?
- Does this lead produce large outdoor or small indoor signs?

A company selling computer aided design (CAD) software, on the other hand, may want to store information like:

- Does the lead use an Apple Mac or a Windows PC?
- Does the lead work in electrical, mechanical, or constructing engineering?

It is important that you can add your own custom fields to the leads database, and that your registration forms can include those to capture this data.

A good marketing automation system should be able to present all information on a lead, and if you are lucky, it uses a nice timeline graph to visualize the lead's activity history graphically in chronological order.

Also, make sure the marketing automation system can define subsets of leads from the complete set, as you will commonly want to do things to leads containing certain filtering criteria. For example, you may want to send an email to leads in a specific country or city, or send a discount offer on red wine only to people who have a shown interest in that.

Automated workflows

A good marketing automation system lets you define flowcharts of custom logic that is triggered automatically when something happens. These events can be a registration form being submitted, an email being opened, or a web page being visited. Once a lead has been enrolled in an automated workflow, the system will follow the rules you have defined and keep doing things related to this particular lead, perhaps for weeks. The workflow can contain *if...else* logic, and alter its behavior based on information from the leads database.

Workflows can perform actions such as sending emails to the lead or notifications to a sales representative. For example, it is common to have leads nurturing workflows that send a series of follow-up emails to new leads or to leads that have submitted a form. The workflows can also contain delays, such that you can control the pace of the actions in the workflow.

Workflows are incredibly powerful and allow you to do various things like:

- Send a set of leads nurturing emails when a lead is created or a web form is submitted
- Send reminder emails if a delivery email or a campaign offer email has not been opened
- Send an email offering an eBook or other educational resources after a lead has visited webpages covering the same topic
- Forward leads notification emails to the sales representative closest to the lead
- Do internal things such as change the value of a status field in the leads database dependent on what the lead is doing on your website

- Send a notification email to yourself when someone has visited your website more than 10 times, read over 50 web pages, or downloaded a specific eBook

The possibilities are nearly endless and come down to your needs and ideas. Just make sure you don't send too many emails to the lead, causing him or her to unregister from further communication. You can usually prevent that by limiting the number of emails to a reasonable level, and by making sure the content is useful and relevant for each lead.

Leads scoring

Leads scoring is a solution to the problem of having too many leads to work on. Some companies get an incredibly large amount of leads and they just don't have resources enough to follow-up with all of them individually.

Automated workflows mentioned above can help to some extent by providing an automatic solution for leads nurturing. However, at some point you may want to call the hottest leads and try to make the sale. Leads scoring try to help with that.

With leads scoring, you define an algorithm that calculates a number indicating how hot a lead is compared to others in your database. Activity on your website gives different scores for different actions. The more activity the lead shows, the higher the score. A simple leads scoring algorithm could, for example, be:

- Reading a blog post gives +1
- Opening a monthly newsletter gives +2
- Each new return visit to your website gives +5
- Submitting a form to read an eBook gives +10
- Attending a webinar training gives +15
- Visiting the pricing page gives +10
- Visiting the job opportunities page gives -5

Depending on how many times this lead has returned to the website, and how many eBooks and webinars have been consumed, the lead will get a number assigned to them indicating their assumed interest level. In reality, it is hard to design a leads scoring system that gives a number that matches the lead's actual interest level, but at least it is a good attempt. If you integrate with a capable video marketing platform (VMP), you can even add video viewing behavior to the leads scoring algorithm.

If you have more leads than you cope with, you may try to define a lead scoring algorithm. It is then common to define a threshold at which the lead is considered a Marketing Qualified Lead (MQL) and is handed over to sales for manual follow-up. Where this threshold is set is also up to you to define.

If you want to use leads scoring, a marketing automation system allows you to define the leads scoring algorithm, and it continuously monitors all the leads and recalculates the score for each one as he or she interacts with your website. The score can be used in automated workflows or other decision logic as well.

Smart content

Do you remember the smart call-to-action button that promoted different types of wine-related offers depending on the visitor's previous activity history? Some marketing automation systems can perform a similar trick for general web page content, like changing the text on a web page. Sometimes this is possible for email content too.

Like the smart call-to-action buttons, smart content can be inserted in web pages such that the information on (parts of) a web page may change based on something the system knows about this visitor.

If information in the leads database indicates this web page visitor has a large yacht or a small one, you can have the web page text change to fit better for people with small or large yachts, instead of the generic default text. Or, say the visitor has spent a lot of time on the windsurfing section of your sports shop website. The introduction text of some web pages may change to something more relevant for people with a windsurfing interest.

The better your offering matches the interests of the website visitor or email reader, the higher the chance of capturing and keeping his or her interest.

CRM integration

The marketing automation system contains a leads database at the core if its functionality, but you may already have a leads database as part of your customer relationship management (CRM) system.

How do they both relate to each other? Should one replace the other? The leads database in the marketing automation system is primarily used for automated marketing efforts and nurturing of leads captured on the Internet, and is most often not suitable to use as your primary CRM system.

The leads database of the CRM system, on the other hand, is primarily geared to manage the manual interactions you have had and plan to have with a lead, as well as recording notes from sales calls and the like. In effect, the leads database in the marketing automation system is suited for all leads, while you may not want to move all relatively cold internet-generated leads into the CRM system.

In most cases, the two leads databases are still needed, as they are targeted for different purposes. But clearly there is an overlapping situation here. Leads in one system may need to be in the other system or vice versa, and additional lead details captured in one of the databases may need to be updated in the other system as well.

Should both systems be synched bi-directionally at all times? Maybe not. My recommendation is to keep the vast amount of unqualified Internet-generated leads in the marketing automation system. Only move them to the CRM database once the leads get the status of being a Marketing Qualified Lead (MQL) for manual follow-up.

A lead entered into the CRM database, on the other hand, should be copied over to the marketing automation system. This is because manually entered leads (perhaps captured at exhibitions or by incoming phone calls) should probably receive some massaging with leads nurturing emails. You also want to be able to track what the lead does on your website onwards.

Keeping both databases updated and in sync manually is a massive undertaking, and in practice it is not doable for anything but tiny leads databases. Therefore, there needs to be an automated synchronization mechanism between the CRM system and marketing automation system you use. The existence of such synchronization bridges may be a major decision factor, and you should check this out carefully prior to buying any marketing automation system.

VMP integration

As video marketing platforms like Wistia and VidYard can generate leads using in-video gating, those leads need to be transferred into the marketing automation system if you want to have everything in one place (and you do).

There are bridges available that solve the problem of synchronizing the leads information between a video marketing platform and a marketing automation system. In addition to the contact information of the lead, detailed statistics on video usage are often synchronized too. It is even possible to let video viewing behavior take part in the leads scoring algorithms or workflow decision logic of your marketing automation system.

The marketing automation system might offer other integrations too, for example to SlideShare.

The Blog engine

A marketing automation system can include a blog engine, which enables you to write blog articles from right within the system, and publish them using the integrated blog hosting system. The advantage is that it is typically easy to add call-to-action buttons and registration forms to the articles as well.

As part of the blog functionality, there should be a WYSIWYG (what you see is what you get) article editor, and a blog front page showing the last ten to fifteen posts in shortened form, as well as the possibility to organize them by topic or author. The blog engine should also contain an article commenting system, and automatic functionality to send instant, daily, weekly, or monthly round-up emails to leads who have registered for that service.

Like everything else, the marketing automation system also tracks the marketing performance of the blog articles, providing statistics on how many times they have been read, what the traffic sources were (links from other web pages, promotions in emails, or organic search traffic, and how many call-to-action clicks triggered a lead to visit a landing page with a registration form.

Emails

Marketing automation systems can usually send two types of emails: mailshots where the same or similar email is sent to many people at the same time, and individual emails sent to one person for a specific reason.

To be more useful and relevant to the recipients, the marketing automation system should allow sending mailshots to more narrowly filtered subsets (segments) of leads. For example, some messages are only sent to the leads from Manhattan who have indicated an interest in attending cooking classes (that you happen to organize in New York). Your leads from San Francisco, Singapore, or London are likely not interested, so don't spam and interrupt them with irrelevant marketing information.

The other type of email is more transactional in its nature, as only one message is sent to a particular lead for a specific purpose, at a certain time. Examples include emails delivering a digital asset once a registration form is submitted, a reminder to open previously delivered and unopened emails, or nurturing emails offering more educational content a few days after the last touch point.

At least basic personalization should be possible in both cases. If you use a good marketing automation system, adaptive smart content can be used to modify parts of the email for each individual lead, based on their specific activity history or other information or criteria. It must also be possible to add images and call-to-action buttons to your email designs.

Good marketing automation systems track the delivery rate and open rates of emails, click-through rates of call-to-action buttons or hyperlinks, and more. In addition to providing information to you in various reports, the system should record it in the leads database for later use in workflow logic or segmentation filters.

Campaigns

Campaigns measure the results of an offer with a specific goal. A campaign can be used to group various activities to measure the combined marketing performance of the offer and to assess how well it achieves its set goal.

For example, you may have developed an eBook on how to buy a family dog. It is promoted using mailshots and your website, blog, and social media with the help of call-to-action buttons, landing pages, and perhaps paid advertisements. You can group all the promotional activities and assets related to that offer in a campaign. The marketing automation system will monitor and meter the marketing performance of the total campaign, letting you know if it creates the amount of visitors, leads, or customers you wanted when the campaign launched.

A campaign can also be used to measure the results of just one marketing activity. The term "campaign" can be anything you want it to be.

Social media integration

Marketing automation systems can include support for management of your social media accounts, which most often includes Facebook, LinkedIn, and Twitter. The functionality varies between different systems, of course, but you can typically post messages and monitor the interactions from within the marketing automation system.

A great feature is to have your new blog posts auto-published to Facebook, LinkedIn, and Twitter at the same time they are published on the blog. This allows you to publish to many social media channels with no extra effort once the blog article is written. The only requirement for this to work is that you use the marketing automation system as your blogging platform.

Website integration

The marketing automation system may host certain services as part of its feature set including the blog, landing pages, or even the full website. In this case, it is easy to insert forms, call-to-action buttons, smart content, and other assets into web pages and blog articles because everything is managed by the same system.

What if you already use other systems for certain parts of your online publishing, for example hosting your website using a different content management system or hosting your blog outside of the marketing automation system?

The trick here is to let the marketing automation system generate a small snippet of HTML/JavaScript code for the objects (call-to-action buttons, forms, etc.) you want to use elsewhere. You can paste this code block into the HTML of a web page or blog article hosted on some other system. That way, the assets of the marketing automation system can be integrated into websites or blogs run outside of it.

Analytics and reporting

Marketing automation systems provide analytics and reporting, helping you to measure and analyze the marketing performance of emails, landing pages, call-to-action buttons, social media channels, and more. Statistical data is presented in easy-to-understand graphs, providing an instant snapshot of your marketing effectiveness.

This enables you to study a wide variety of useful statistics on how various pieces of your online marketing system perform, including cross-tabulated data on different types of data points.

Chapter summary

In this chapter, we have discussed what marketing automation systems can do, including visitor and leads activity tracking, landing pages with smart registration forms, workflows and email distribution, personalized content, leads scoring, and more.

The next chapter will provide information on how to do A/B testing to optimize your marketing results.

Optimizing results with A/B testing

A/B testing is an important concept in Internet marketing. It is a simple technique, where two alternate versions of something are tested against each other during a certain time. After the test, it is assessed if version A or version B performed best. The winning version is then used going forward.

If you use a fully integrated marketing automation system, it likely includes features for automatic A/B testing of emails, call-to-action buttons, and landing pages. A/B testing can be done manually, but it is usually more complicated and cumbersome, and in practice it may be impractical without tool support.

Emails

A/B testing of emails means the mailing system may send the first 10% of the emails in a mail shot using two different versions (A and B) to half of the test group each. Dependent on which version got the highest open or click rate in the initial test run, the remaining 90% of the emails are sent using the winning version.

In the example above, only 5% of the recipients get to see the lower-performing email version, while 95% get to see the version that interest readers more. This is a small tradeoff compared to getting the majority of recipients to engage to a higher degree.

Web pages, banner ads, and calls-to-action

The same A/B testing approach can be done for CTA buttons, banner ads, or landing pages. Two versions are prepared and tested in parallel during some initial time span, and the winning version (the one that triggered most clicks or form submissions) is used onwards.

You can repeat the A/B testing multiple times, and challenge the new winner with yet another version. This can be repeated as many times as you like, but you will need to have traffic enough to gather conclusive test results without waiting too long.

If you do not have a marketing automation system or some other system to perform A/B testing, a free solution is provided by Google Analytics, which we'll discuss later.

Other companies like Optimizely also offer solutions for A/B testing: **https://www.optimizely.com**

Chapter summary

In this chapter, we have discussed how A/B testing of emails, calls-to-action and landing pages can be used to optimize the marketing performance. In the next chapter, we will look into web analytics.

Web analytics 1 - Measure and improve

In Internet marketing, even small changes can make a big difference. Therefore, you should continuously monitor the performance of your website and related marketing efforts, analyze the results, and improve as needed.

How do you analyze a website's performance so you can improve it? Content management systems like WordPress or Joomla can show page view statistics, which is a start, but there is something much better than just using the page view counts. That is to use a powerful web analytics tool that can provide in-depth information on how the website performs and how the visitors use it.

Web analytics tools

There are two types of web analytics tools available: client-side page tag tools and server-side log file tools. They both provide detailed data on how your website performs and is being used, but they work in different ways.

Client-side page tag tools

With this type of tool, you need to adjust each HTML page on the website with a JavaScript code snippet (the page tag) to record whenever the web page has been viewed.

The JavaScript code sends information to a remote server, usually hosted by a Software as a Service (SaaS) supplier. The data-collecting server stores the web metrics data and provides data visualization capabilities. This type of solution requires the use of tracking cookies, for example, to record if a website user is a new or returning visitor.

Client-side page tag tools are the most common solution and are convenient, since no software needs to be installed and maintained on the web server. The downside is that these tools can only analyze data from the time of instrumentation onwards.

Potential problems with page tag tools are implementation errors (for example, pages without a page tag or JavaScript execution errors), and rejected or deleted cookies. Firewalls preventing the page tags to send data back to the analysis server can also cause problems.

Server-side log file tools

With this type of tool, no instrumentation is needed in the HTML pages. Instead, software that analyzes the webserver log files is installed on the server. Therefore, you can analyze website usage also for historical data, provided the log files still contain this data.

Unless these tools use cookies as well, server-side log file analysis suffers from the problem of dynamically assigned IP addresses used by many Internet Service Providers (ISPs). With dynamically assignment, the IP address cannot be used to identify a returning user.

Another problem is page caching, where a web page is sometimes cached on the visitor's computer or using some intermediate web accelerator technology. In this case, the web server does not get a page view at all, thus skewing the web metrics as well.

Google Analytics

Google Analytics is an advanced web analytics tool offered for free, and thanks to its power and zero cost, it is used by the majority of websites today. It is a client-side page tag tool and thus relies on tracking cookies and JavaScript code instrumentation being added to all the pages on your site.

If your website does not already use Google Analytics, I strongly recommend starting now. The only thing you need to do is to register for a free account with Google Analytics and paste the provided HTML/JavaScript tracking code into all your web pages.

Rather than pasting the tracking code into many web pages manually, you can usually do this as a global setting for the whole website. You do this in the administration panel of the content management system. This saves you a lot of work, and there is no risk of forgetting to instrument some pages.

Once you have instrumented all the web pages with the Google Analytics tracking code, you can log in to Google Analytics and get incredibly detailed statistics on everything related to how your visitors use the site. You can track where they come from, how long they stay, what they do, how they move, and where they leave.

Google Analytics can show you a lot of information on your audience, for example the age and gender of visitors, their geographical location, language settings, and computer platform. You can also track metrics like the number of visitors, return visits, and duration of visits, as well as trend and search keyword analysis. There is also goal conversion, campaign, event, and social media tracking.

Google Analytics even provides a real-time mode, visualizing usage data as it happens. This can be useful when debugging your website or Google Analytics integration, as data generally show up in other types of reports many hours after the visitor engagement happened. This delay makes it difficult to see the results of your testing.

Additionally, Google Analytics provides means to integrate with other online and offline data sources, providing a centralized view of everything related to your website marketing performance. This can resolve the common problem of having data scattered over a number of monitoring tools, or even not having the data available for analysis at all.

Some of the more advanced marketing automation systems provide web analytics to some degree too, but they tend to focus on higher-level metrics, often related to the tracking of individual identified leads or customers. Google Analytics goes into much more detail, but only works on statistics for all visitors or segmented parts of your user base, not individual identified visitors.

The main problem with Google Analytics is that it is almost too good—it provides so much data it can be overwhelming to new users. Thus, some guidance is needed for new users to help them understand the capabilities at their disposal. In short, it is easy not to see the forest through the trees.

This book does not teach you the capabilities of any other software product, but as Google Analytics is so important, I make an exception and will explain some if its features. They are important to any website owner.

This is by no means a complete overview of Google Analytics, and there are many capabilities not mentioned here. We won't cover how to use it in detail, but will provide an overview of some of its more interesting features of value to most readers. You may want to check out YouTube or the Google Analytics Academy for free training resources:
http://analyticsacademy.withgoogle.com
https://analyticsacademy.withgoogle.com/explorer/resour
ces

With that said, let's dive in and see what it can do.

Basic metrics

When you log in to Google Analytics, select the website you want to analyze (you probably only have one to choose from at this time). You are then presented with the main report (also accessible using the menu option [Audience > Overview]).

This audience overview report provides the most important general statistics. In the top right corner, you can select what date range you want to analyze. You can define any range you like, and you can also change the detail of the main graph using the Hourly/Day/Week/Month buttons. These settings are available in most reports throughout Google Analytics.

The main graph in this report shows the number of website visits (also called sessions) over time. The small miniature graphs are called sparklines and show additional data for the selected date range.

Sessions

Sessions are the total number of individual visitor sessions on your website, i.e. the number of visits. If a user has been inactive 30 minutes or more, any future activity will be considered a new visit. Vice versa, a user who leaves your website and come back within 30 minutes is considered the same visit.

Having a high number of sessions/visits means you get a lot of traffic to the website. However, it doesn't say anything about the quality of the traffic, or if you have few visitors returning often or many new visitors who never return.

Users

Users are the total number of unique users visiting your website. Having a high number of users means there are many people who find an interest in coming to your website, but it does not say anything about the quality of those visitors.

This figure is not as accurate as you may want. For example, the same visitor can use multiple devices to access your website, or clean the tracking cookies occasionally. In this case, the same user is erroneously reported as different users. Multiple people may use the same computer, causing the opposite effect.

Pageviews

Pageviews is the total number of web pages viewed by all visitors in total. Multiple views are counted; if a unique user visit the same web page several times, the pageview count will be increased by one each time.

Pages/session

Pages/session is the average number of web pages viewed per visit. This is also called the depth of the visit. The pages/session ratio is more interesting than the pageview count, as it shows how many pages each visitor views on average.

Having a high pages/session ratio means your visitors stay to read more content. In short, it is a measure of how interesting your visitors think your website is.

Average session duration

Average session duration is the average time each website visitor spends on the website before leaving. In analogy to the visit depth mentioned above, this is also called the visit duration. A higher value means your visitors find your website of interest and stay longer.

Bounce rate

Bounce rate is the percentage of visitors who come to your website, only view the page they arrive at, and leave without taking any further actions. Essentially, bounce rate is the percentage of sessions that are one-page only visits.

A high value could mean the page they came to contained all the information they needed, but is it not the best interpretation. More likely, the page was not of any use to the visitor at all, causing him or her to leave immediately. In either case, there was nothing on the page that enticed them to stay longer and explore other pages on the website. A high bounce rate is generally considered a bad thing.

% new sessions

% new sessions are the percentage of visitors who have not been on your website before, i.e. the share of new versus returning visitors. You may think it is good your website gets many new visitors, and it is, but it is also not good if your visitors don't come back.

Therefore, you don't want this measure to be in either of the extreme ends, but rather somewhere in the middle. Perhaps you want it to be tilted a bit in either direction, depending on if your aim is customer loyalty or growth. Just like the number of unique visitors above, this measure will be skewed if users clean their cookies or use multiple devices, erroneously reporting repeat visitors as new visitors.

Other metrics

Below the main graph and the smaller sparkline graphs, there is an area with more detailed information in text format.

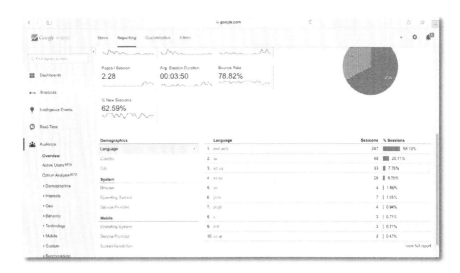

In the left column are Demographics, System, and Mobile groups, while the right column contains detailed data from the selected option in the left column.

- Demographics - display what language your visitors use, and what country and city they are located in.

- System – display what web browser, operating system, and Internet service provider your visitors use.

- Mobile - display what screen resolution your visitors have on their mobile devices, as well as the operating system and Internet service provider in use.

In addition to the main audience overview report outlined above, there are many other reports in Google Analytics providing a wealth of useful and detailed information. In fact, Google Analytics has over 100 reports with a multitude of options, segmentation, and cross-referencing capabilities.

It would be a full-time job to monitor them all continuously. I recommend starting with a few that make most sense for your business objectives. Over time, add new reports as you get additional skills. In the following sections, I outline a number of the capabilities of Google Analytics.

The list is by no means complete but shows the analytics power Google provides to you for free. If you are completely new to Google Analytics and web metrics in general, you may be surprised to see what insights can be made by mining statistical data with these tools.

Demographics

Google Analytics is capable of providing a lot of information on the demographics of your users, including their geographical location, language, sex, and age. Dependent on your business, this may or may not be of importance for your marketing strategies.

Language

Using the Language report [Audience > Geo > Language], you can see detailed information on what language settings your website visitors have in their computer, and how their visitor behavior differs because of it.

For example, you may find you have many Spanish-speaking visitors, and that they have a much higher bounce rate or lower visit durations than other users. Perhaps it could be worthwhile to provide a special website section in Spanish to accommodate this group.

Location

Using the Location report [Audience > Geo > Location], you can see where your visitors come from, and how their visitor behavior differs depending on location. This can provide guidelines on where marketing efforts may give the best return.

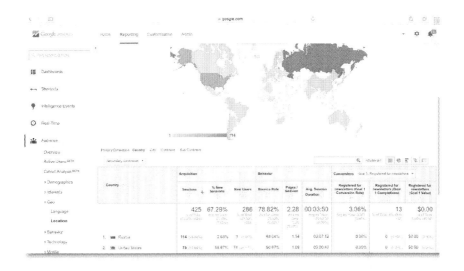

By default, the report shows the total number of sessions from each location. The geographical charts are heat maps, so the density of users is shown using color intensity. You can immediately provide a quick graphical overview of where your visitors come from.

Using the Session drop-down list in the top left part of the map area (outside the visible area in the screenshot above), you can analyze the bounce rate or average session duration from different regions, for example. In the image below, the map shows the bounce rate rather than the number of visits (the drop-down list is visible here, now with a Bounce rate label).

As you can see, the user behavior in terms of visits and bounce rate is quite different in various countries.

You can drill down from continents to country, state, and city level to analyze website behavior from increasingly narrow geographical segments of visitors.

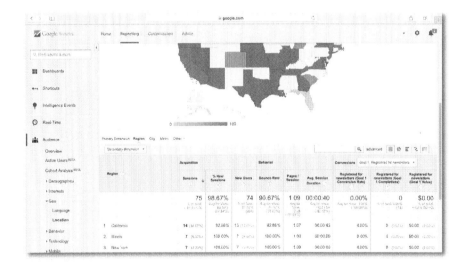

You can also study the details using the tabular data below the charts, or change from tabular format to different types of graphical charts using the visualization mode buttons (to the right of the search field).

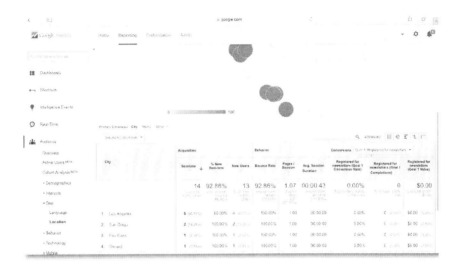

Sex and age

Google Analytics can provide information on age and sex of your website users, although this capability is disabled if your website has too little traffic. This is to protect the privacy of visitors on low-traffic websites.

Use the Sex or Age reports if you want to analyze this, found at [Audience > Demographics > Sex] and [Audience > Demographics > Age].

Website usage

Understanding where visitors enter your website, how they move, and where they leave is critical in designing and optimizing performance. If you notice a large part of your visitors arrive at an unexpected entry page, make sure its content is suited for being the first page a new visitor will see.

Vice versa, if many visitors leave your site from a certain web page, look into this and try to understand what it is on this page that makes them leave. Try to rework the page and make it keep visitors if you can.

Which pages should be improved first? What pages need better visibility in menus or by other means? All these questions can be answered by using Google Analytics.

Understanding the user flow

You can get incredibly valuable user flow statistics using the Users flow report [Audience > Users Flow]. There you can see how visitors arrive (by default segmented by country), how they move, and what pages trigger them to leave the website.

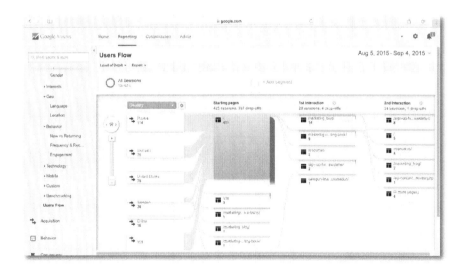

Each green box in the chart represents one web page on your website. Gray arrows of different width connect the pages, visualizing the user flow. The fatter the arrow, the more visitors move along that path. The red pipe to the right of the green page boxes shows how many visitors you lose on that page. The larger the red pipe, the more visitors leave the website there.

If you click the left mouse button on any of the web pages (green boxes) in the chart, a popup menu appears. Select "Highlight traffic through here" to more easily see where the traffic came from and went because traffic flows irrelevant to this page are dimmed out.

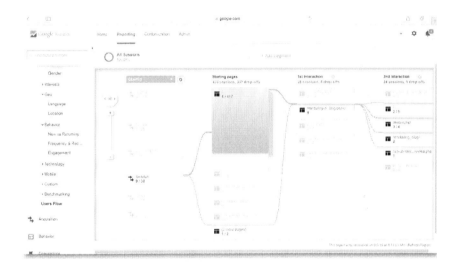

If you instead use the menu command "Explore traffic through here", you can see where the traffic came from and went, with the selected page as the center of the universe. This makes it easier to understand the user flow of a particular web page.

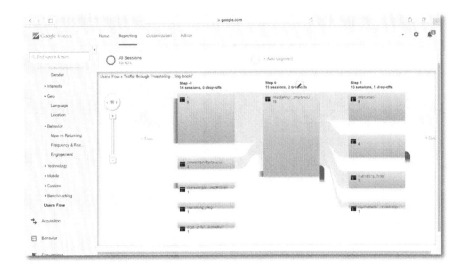

Again, pay attention to the red pipes to the right of the green page boxes. This is where you lose visitors.

Where do visitors enter?

To get a better overview of what pages are the most common ones to enter your website, you can use the Landing Pages report [Behavior > Site Content > Landing Pages]. Here you get a sorted list of the most common entry pages, making it easy to see what pages need to be adapted to be most effective as the first page a new website visitor sees.

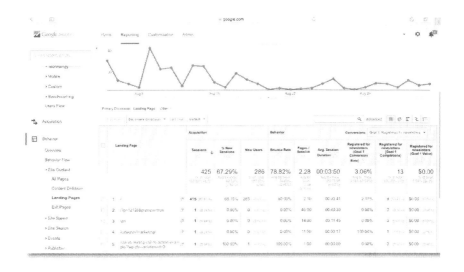

In particular, ensure no popular entry pages have a high bounce rate, as this implies new users leave immediately. If so, review the underperforming entry page and try to make it keep the new visitors. You spent a lot of effort to get visitors, don't scare them off right away.

Where do visitors exit?

On the other hand, if you want to see what pages are most commonly the last one viewed before visitors leave your website, use the "Exit pages" report [Behavior > Site Content > Exit Pages].

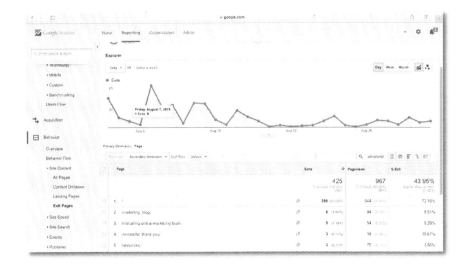

In this report, you get a sorted list of the most common exit pages. This provides the means to see what pages needs to be improved so they don't continue to lose as many visitors.

What pages are most popular?

When optimizing a website, it is important to spend time making sure the most popular web pages are perfected. It is of less use to have fantastic design and content on your least viewed pages if your most popular pages are not at their best. Spend time improving the layout and content of pages with many visitors first, and worry about low-traffic pages later.

In particular, make sure your most popular pages have call-to-action buttons that entice the visitor to register their contact information in a landing page form, or continue down the customer journey in some other way.

Use the All Pages report [Behavior > Site Content > All Pages] to get a sorted list of the most viewed pages on your website.

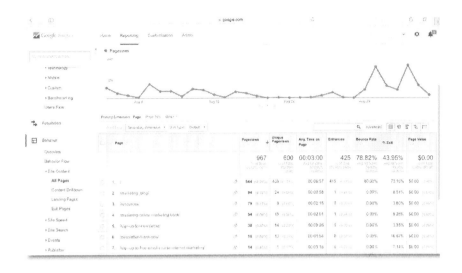

It is the top ones that you should review and possibly improve first, as they have the most readers. Any improvement in design or content on them will benefit many visitors and improve your results immediately.

What pages are least popular?

The least visited pages with few views are subject to another type of analysis: why doesn't anyone read them?

Are they difficult to find in the menu system, or is the heading not right? Perhaps the topic is not relevant for the readers of the website? You may need to do more promotion of the page by adding more hypertext links to it from other pages, or call-to-action buttons promoting it.

You can find the least viewed pages by clicking on the Pageviews column header in the All Pages report [Behavior > Site Content > All Pages]. This sorts the pages by reversed pageviews order.

Try to understand why many visitors do not want to read the unpopular pages, and rectify the situation if you can.

While we're at it, we can also check what pages have the highest bounce rate. These are the pages with the least engagement (visitors arrive at the page but leave without any further action). You can check this by clicking on the Bounce Rate column header in the All Pages report.

By listing the pages with the highest bounce rate, you can see what pages interest your readers the least. For any page with 50% bounce rate or more, review why this is the case. Perhaps the topic is irrelevant, out-of-date, or there are other problems with it. If you can't find a reason, consider removing it, as it might not add any value to your website.

Pages with a bounce rate in the range of 25% to 50% are good candidates for improvement. This means visitors read them, but you can probably optimize them to increase visitor engagement.

In-page click analysis

With the In-Page Analytics report [Behavior > In-page Analytics], you can see the number of clicks different hyperlinks have as an overlay on a particular page. This gives you a graphical way of understanding what hyperlinks are clicked the most on a certain page.

Visitor statistics

Google Analytics provides the means to understand visitor behavior, and compare it between different types of user groups (segments). Use this to improve your understanding of visitor behavior.

New versus returning visitors

Using the New Versus Returning report [Audience > Behavior > New vs Returning], you can see the ratio between new and repeat visitors. You can also see detailed information on how the behavior is different for new and returning visitors respectively.

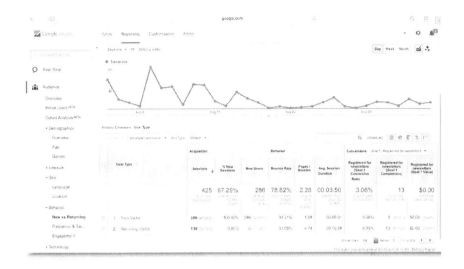

While it is a good thing to get many new visitors, it is not good to have few return visits. This indicates the website does not provide enough value for a second or third visit later. What constitutes a good balance is largely up to your organization to define, depending on if you focus on growth or loyalty.

Frequency and Recency

The Frequency and Recency report [Audience > Behavior > Frequency & Recency] shows how website visitors return to the website.

The default panel of this report show how often visitors come back to your website (the frequency). In other words, it shows how many repeat visits there were in the defined time range, and the number of sessions and pageviews there have been for the visitors of different frequency.

The first row in the table shows the amount of visits from users who have only been on your website once. The second row shows the number of visits from users who have been on your website twice, and so on.

If a user returns to a website multiple times in the given time range, they are counted each time. For example, if a visitor makes their first and second visit in the period, they will be counted both in the first and second row, as they both made a first visit and second visit in the defined time range.

By selecting the Days Since Last Session panel of this report, you get to see when users making visits within the given time range last visited your website.

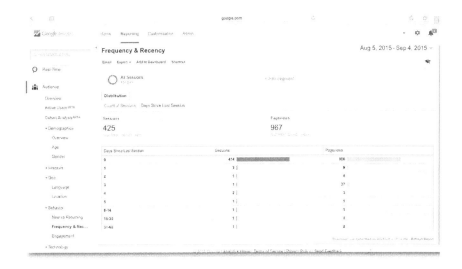

The first row shows the amount of visitors that have returned within the same day from their previous visit. This value is skewed because it also contains the number of one-time visits without any return visits.

The second row contains the number of visitors that had their previous visit one day before, the third row shows the number of users that had a previous visit two days earlier, and so on. A high recency is better than a low one, as the fewer days there is between visits, the higher the engagement.

Engagement

Use the Engagement report [Audience > Behavior > Engagement] to see how long visitors stay on your website, and how that affects their behavior. For each row in the table, you can see the number of sessions and pageviews for visitors staying for the duration of the time span defined in that row.

What technology do your visitors use?

Using the Browser and OS report [Audience > Technology > Browser & OS], you can see a lot of detailed information on what systems and technology your website visitors use.

By default, the Browser panel is listed. It shows what browsers your visitors have and how their behavior is different.

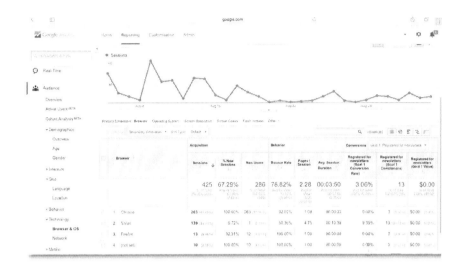

By clicking on the Operating System link, the corresponding panel is displayed, showing detailed information on what operating systems your visitors use.

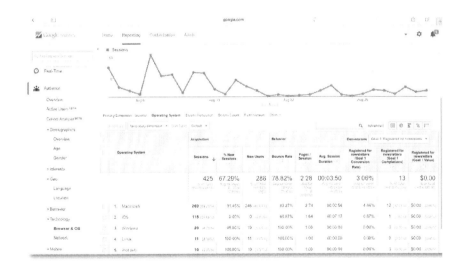

Other panels in this report show additional data.

How mobile are your users?

Using the Mobile Overview report [Audience > Mobile > Overview], you can see how many of your visitors use a desktop computer, smartphone, or tablet to access your website.

Using the Mobile Devices report [Audience > Mobile > Devices], you can even see what mobile devices (brand and model) your visitors use to access your website.

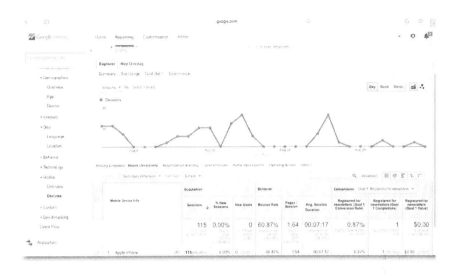

Where do visitors come from?

It is often interesting to see where your traffic comes from, both on an overview level and in some more detail. Google Analytics provides a number of reports and capabilities that provide detailed information on this.

Traffic sources

The sources generating the most traffic can be viewed using the Channel report [Acquisition > All Traffic > Channels]. Here you can see how much of your traffic is direct or arrives thanks to search engines (organic traffic), social media, or referrals from other websites.

What is direct traffic anyway? It means Google could not track where it came from. This could be due to many things, for example:

- The URL was typed directly into the web browser address field
- A click on a hyperlink in a PDF or other document
- A click on a hyperlink in an email
- A click on a web browser bookmark linking to your website

In short, the channels report provides the top-level overview of where your visitors come from.

Referrals

It is interesting to see what other websites send traffic to you. This can be analyzed using the Referrals report [Acquisition > All Traffic > Referrals].

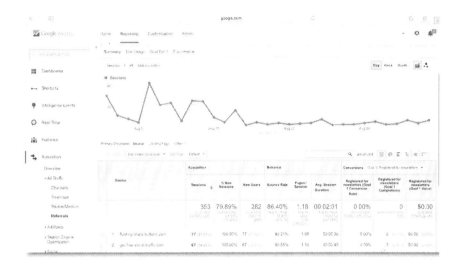

This report displays what external websites send most traffic to you, along with additional traffic data for each one.

User segmentation

Understanding how visitors behave on the website is key to optimizing the marketing performance. Up to now, all Google Analytics reports I have described have shown data for all visitors. But showing visitors as a homogenous group may not be sufficient. Sometimes it is necessary to break down the information and analyze how different groups behave. This is segmentation.

Segmenting your visitors lets you analyze their behavior based on attributes like geographical location, language, what technology they use, how they engage with the website, and more. Segmentation can be broad (like new versus returning visitors) or narrow (such as visitors from Germany who arrived from a Google search using an iPhone).

Selecting and comparing segments

Most of the reports in Google Analytics allow you to select what segment of visitors to visualize, or to compare different segmentations. By default, the reports show All Sessions, as shown in the Audience Overview report below.

To show data from one or more particular segments of users, click All Sessions above the main graph. You can then select which of the predefined user segmentations you want to visualize in the report.

Perhaps you want to compare all sessions to bounced sessions, direct traffic, and mobile visitors? If so, select the corresponding checkboxes as shown in the screenshot below.

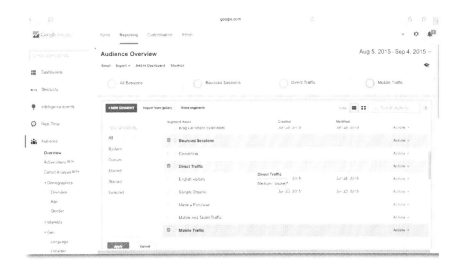

Click the Apply button. The report will now show comparative data for the selected segments of users, making it easy to understand how the behavior differs in different groups of visitors.

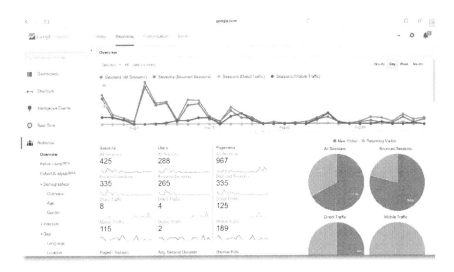

By selecting or comparing different segments of users, you can easily understand how website usage differs for certain groups. This can lead to important insights to help adjust your marketing approach.

Creating custom segments

To create a new custom segment, go to any of the reports that allow segmentation filtering (for example the Audience Overview report). Then click the Add Segment button.

You can either import readymade segmentation definitions or create a new custom segment definition.

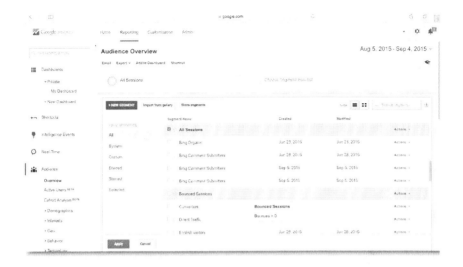

If you chose to import a predefined segment definition, click the Import from Gallery button. You can now select a segmentation definition from the library.

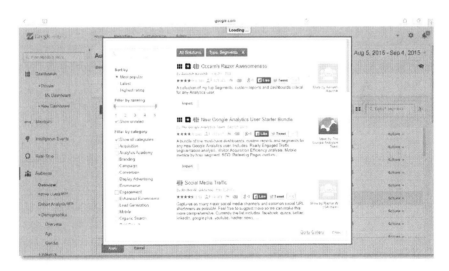

Alternatively, click the "New Segment" button and define your own visitor segmentation instead. Your segmentation definition can include users with certain:

- Demographics (sex, age, location, language)
- Technology (operating system, browser, mobile device model)
- Behavior (number of sessions, duration, time since last visit)
- Traffic sources (campaign, medium, source)

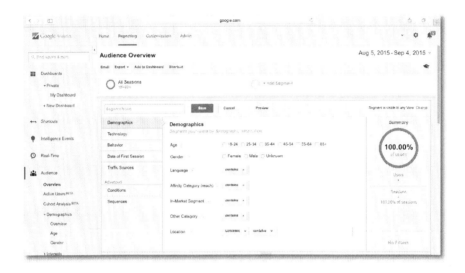

Define the user selection you want, click Save, and the new user segmentation can be used for visualization or comparisons in the different reports.

Chapter summary

This chapter gave an introduction to web metrics using Google Analytics, explaining how you can measure and optimize website user behavior. The next chapter will continue with additional information on how you can measure goals and campaign results using Google Analytics.

Web analytics 2 - Monitor results

The previous chapter looked at how Google Analytics can be used to understand what visitors you have, how they behave, how the website performs, and how it can be improved.

This chapter is about understanding the marketing results of your website and other marketing efforts on a higher level of abstraction.

Goals and KPIs

Google Analytics records a massive amount of data, and it can be daunting to browse it all to get the information you need to make the right decisions. Nor should you try. By defining goals, you can track how well your website performs on the most important key parameters (or Key Performance Indicators, KPIs) of your organization.

Goals let you easily measure how well the website converts visitors into leads or buyers, subscribers, video watchers, or whatever your goals are. In short, goals measure how well business objectives are achieved. There are two types of goal conversions:

- Macro conversions
- Micro conversions

Macro conversions are the top-level objectives of the website (for example getting a purchase in the webshop, or get a subscriber to a blog), while micro conversions are smaller goals (such as reading a whitepaper or viewing a product video) that happen on the way to the macro conversion.

Micro conversions are important because they help building a relationship with the potential customer that can ultimately lead to the macro conversion, and the macro conversion may never happen unless the micro conversion is completed first.

Another way to define a goal in the context of website metrics is that a goal is a pageview of greater value than most others, such as arriving at a thank you page after signing up for a webinar, for example.

Google Analytics can track any goal you define, and thus accommodate both micro and macro conversion goal setting and monitoring. Measuring goal completions using Google Analytics is a good way to provide the feedback loop for the goals and KPIs you should have defined earlier.

Setting goals

When you set goals, it is important to consider what your objectives are. Do you want to make sales, create leads, get subscribers, quote requests, reduce the number of support questions, or something else? To create a goal in Google Analytics, go to the Admin > Goals panel.

Click on the New Goal button. In the next panel, you can choose a goal definition from readymade templates, or create a new one. If you decide to create a custom goal, you can select one of several predefined goal types:

- A specific page or website section has been visited
- A visitor has stayed a certain duration
- A number of pages/visit has been passed
- An event has been triggered (see the next chapter)

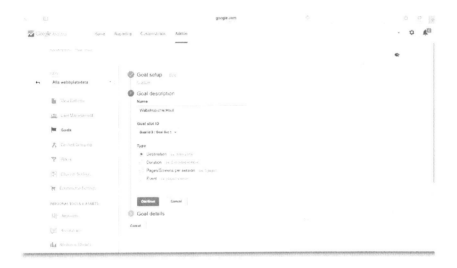

The most common goal is to track if a user has visited a certain web page or not. In the example below, a goal is defined to be fulfilled when a user has visited the webshop checkout page (shown as /checkout).

You can specify a particular page name (exact match), any page on a subsection of your website (head match), or any page that matches a certain name pattern (regular expression match).

A goal can optionally have a value and a funnel defined to it as well.

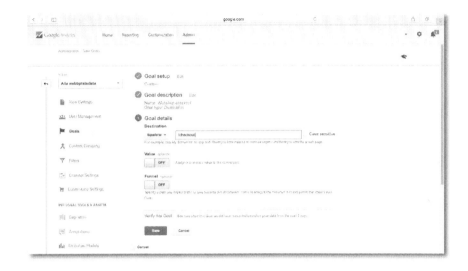

A funnel is a stepwise view of the pages expected to be visited before the goal is fulfilled, for example, the checkout process in a web shop, or a hotel booking wizard at a booking site. The purpose of defining a funnel is to analyze how many visitors arrive and drop-off at the various steps leading up to the goal being fulfilled.

A goal value can help estimate the expected income by measuring how many times the goals are fulfilled by your visitors. This only works if you know what average value a goal conversion has. Assume for example 10% of the visitors who download your brochure end up buying a product at an average value of 50 USD. Then the goal value for a brochure download is 50/10 = 5 USD.

Often, you have no value information for goals. You can then use the goal value to set the relative importance of different goals, for example, 1 USD for visiting the pricing page and 10 USD for signing up for your product demonstration webinar. While the values have no meaning in absolute numbers, they can show the relative success of different goals.

Goal results

Once one or more goals are defined, you can see how well they perform depending on what visitors do on the website. Use the Goals Overview report [Conversions > Goals > Overview] to analyze results.

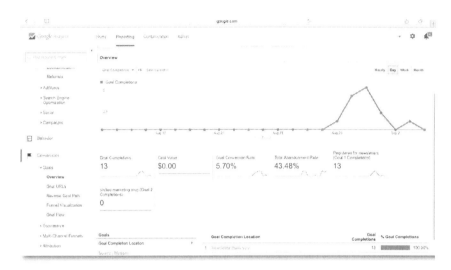

The main graph visualizes the total number of goals achieved each day along with other top-level data like total goal value and goal conversion rate. Beneath the main goal-completion graph, detailed data is available for each of your defined goals.

Goal funnels - the expected path

As mentioned, a goal can optionally have a funnel defined to it. The funnel is the set of web pages a visitor is supposed to visit before the goal is fulfilled. Assume for example you have a landing page with a registration form that offers an eBook PDF. The goal is accomplished when the visitor has submitted the registration form and is redirected to the thank you page (i.e. the eBook has been downloaded).

While downloading the eBook is your goal in the general sense, technically this is most easily tracked by defining a visit to the thank you page as the goal. Visiting the landing page with the form guarding access to the eBook is the only step in the funnel leading up to this goal. Other multi-page funnels can include membership registrations, a bank account application, or the checkout steps in a web shop. A funnel can be any stepwise sequence of pages that makes sense for you to monitor.

To visualize the funnel of any goal, use the Funnel Visualization report [Conversions > Goals > Funnel Visualization] and select the goal of interest (it must be defined previously). This report will show the funnel steps (set of pages) the visitor is expected to pass sequentially to arrive at the goal. Provided you have defined a funnel for this goal, of course.

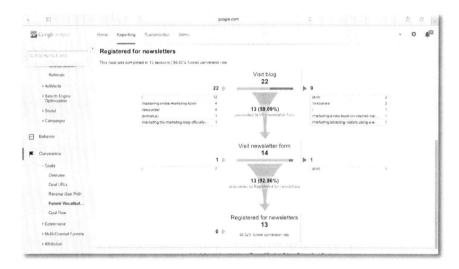

At the top of the funnel, many visitors arrive at the first basket. For each step into the funnel, some visitors drop off and a smaller group continues to the next step. Google Analytics shows where the visitors come from (left side), where they leave to (right side), and how many continue to the next funnel step (going down).

The Funnel Visualization report is key to understanding where visitors abandon the funnel, and therefore fail to fulfill your goal. For any funnel step (page) that loses many visitors, try to understand why and see if you can change it to perform better. Perhaps a web form asks too many intimidating questions, for example.

You want your goals to generate real value and that only happens if the visitors complete the funnel. A visitor leaving the funnel instead of completing the goal is a lost opportunity.

Reverse goal paths - the actual paths

The funnel is the route you think visitors should take to fulfill a goal, but sometimes visitors enter the funnel and goal conversion paths in unexpected ways. The reverse goal path report answers the question: "If visitors arrived at this funnel step, where did they come from?"

Visualize this using the Reverse Goal Path report [Conversions > Goals > Reverse Goal Path].

For each goal, you can see the routes visitors have actually taken to enter the funnel and fulfill the goal.

Goal flow - the detailed view

The Goal flow report [Conversions > Goals > Goal Flow] shows funnel steps including loops, and also helps you find unanticipated user flows.

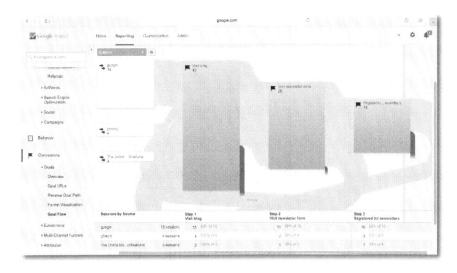

Using this report, you can find out what the visitors are doing in detail. The goal flow path report includes all the paths around the website that involve the pages in the funnel of a particular goal, including loops.

This report may reveal problems in the funnel. For example, you may detect that many visitors move back to an earlier funnel step due to unclear or confusing information.

Campaign monitoring

Since Google Analytics offers such a large amount of information related to the activities on your website, you may also want to get a better understanding of the results of all your online or offline marketing campaigns in one place.

You can track how many leads or customers your different online ads or marketing campaigns generate. If you set things up right, this is also possible for offline marketing such as ads in print media, TV/radio, on your company van, stickers on your delivered products, or flyers you hand out at exhibitions.

How are disparate online and offline marketing campaign results combined with other online web metrics to produce a combined view, enabling you to get valuable insights from disconnected marketing channels? At first, it appears impossible to integrate offline campaign data into Google Analytics. How can this possibly be done?

Measuring online and offline campaigns

Google Analytics provides the capability to tag traffic in custom ways, thanks to something called UTM parameters. This can be used to implement efficient campaign tracking for both online and offline marketing campaigns, like Facebook ads, brochures handed out at events, or print ads in your local newspaper.

Using UTM parameters, you can add custom data sources and marketing channels to Google Analytics tracking. It thus becomes possible to analyze the results of specific email shots, online ads, or offline marketing campaigns that drive traffic to one or more web pages on your site.

While adding campaign tags to your website using UTM parameters may sound complicated, nothing is further from the truth. You only need to modify the inbound links for the landing page URLs and add some additional data to them.

For example, assume you want to track the results of a specific Facebook ad, or an offline ad in your local newspaper driving traffic to a landing page on your website. The landing page the ads drive traffic to (using hyperlinks for the online ads and a printed URL in the offline ad) is called: www.example.com/springcampaign.

To get Google Analytics to track the ad (or more generically, the campaign) separately, you simply add a few details (called UTM campaign tags) to the end of the landing page URL. This helps Google Analytics to understand how visitors got to your website.

In short, UTM tags allow you to design hypertext links that include information on what ad or campaign triggered the user to visit the website. The parameters that must be added to the landing page URL are:

- utm_source: The campaign source (such as Facebook, the January newsletter, or the New York Times). This is where the visitor arrives from.

- utm_medium: The campaign medium (e.g. Social media, newsletter email, or print ad). This is the type of marketing channel that triggered the visit.

- utm_campaign: The campaign name (such as "spring discount" campaign, or "product X launch" campaign, "new subscriber discount" campaign).

These parameters can be used on an optional basis:

- utm_content: You can also add and track campaign details to differentiate what specific ad version or what hyperlink in an email generated traffic to the landing page, for example.

- *utm_term: If you use paid advertisement solutions, this parameter describes the search term that triggered the engagement.

For Google Analytics to be able to track campaign specific results, the online or offline ads should instead drive traffic to a landing page with the UTM tag parameters added, like so:

http://www.example.com/springcampaign?utm_source=Print%20media&utm_medium=Newspaper&utm_campaign=New%20York%20Times%20ads&utm_content=Sports%20car%20ad

The characters in boldface are the custom medium, source, campaign, and content labels defined by you (these will be visible in the Google Analytics reports). The %20 tokens in the tagged URL represent a space character, making space-separated multi-word labels possible in the Google Analytics reports.

The above UTM tagged landing page URL will record the following data in Google Analytics:

Source	Medium	Campaign	Content
Print media	Newspaper	New York Times ads	Sports car ad

To make it easy to create correctly formed UTM tagged URLs, Google even provides a link builder tool. You can be find it here—just enter the suitable data in the form fields and click the Generate URL button to get the UTM tagged version automatically:
https://support.google.com/analytics/answer/1033867?rd=2

Unfortunately, the UTM tagged URL is a bit cumbersome for your visitors to use. For online ads, this is not so much of a problem, as you define the ad on-click link only once.

But for offline campaigns, like ads in print media or TV/radio ads driving traffic to your landing pages, you cannot expect your potential customers to type the rather complicated URL. Furthermore, any spelling mistake would mess up the recorded metrics.

The trick is to let your web developer setup a URL redirect, in effect creating a shorter virtual URL that you publish and promote in offline ads. Once used, the virtual, normal-looking URL automatically redirects the visitor to the real landing page with the UTM campaign tags added.

For example, you can setup the following URL as a redirect:
http://www.example.com/promotion

Whenever someone tries to visit that non-existent virtual page, the webserver automatically redirects them to the UTM campaigned tagged real landing page:
http://www.example.com/springcampaign?utm_source=Print%20med ia&utm_medium=Newspaper&utm_campaign=New%20York%20Tim es%20ads&utm_content=Sports%20car%20ad

This little trick enables you to promote a reasonably short landing page URL in offline media while at the same time leveraging the longer-form UTM campaign tagging parameters to record any online or offline campaign results.

Analyzing campaign results

Now that you have setup UTM tagged landing page URLs to track various online and offline traffic sources, you want to analyze the results. Perhaps you have questions like these:

- How many visitors came from your ad in the local printed newspaper last week?
- How many eBooks were downloaded as a result of your last mailshot?
- How many leads did you get as a result of the promotion you had in the local radio station?
- What were the results from the stickers you handed out at the last exhibition?
- Do you get any visitors from the company van signage?

Questions like these can be answered using the Google Analytics campaign monitoring capabilities. To view the results of your custom (UTM tagged) campaigns, as well as Google AdWords paid advertisement campaigns, use the All Campaigns report [Acquisition > Campaigns > All Campaigns].

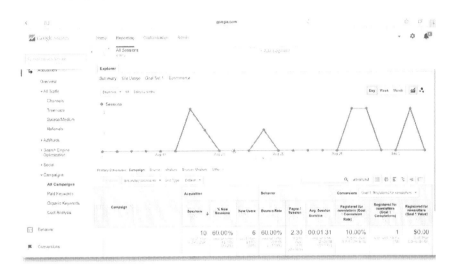

This report lists all the campaigns recorded by Google Analytics, along with traffic statistics, goal completion, and goal value information for each of them. You can drill down into any campaign for increased detail.

In the example below, I clicked the New York Times Ads campaign. Google Analytics will now show what sources and mediums were responsible for generating the traffic for this campaign.

In the example above, we can see the New York Times Ads campaign received traffic from both an offline print ad as well as from an online banner ad on the newspaper website.

Dashboards

With all that data available for visualization and analysis, it might be cumbersome to get an at-a-glance picture of the most relevant metrics and KPIs. You are probably drenched in data by this point. Luckily, Google Analytics allows you to create one or more dashboards with a custom setup of report data, making it easier to get a top-level picture of the current state.

Find your custom dashboards under the [Dashboards > Private] menu option. Select any of them to view the specific data collected on that dashboard.

To add custom dashboards, use the [Dashboards > New Dashboard] menu option. Name the new dashboard, and proceed using one of the options:

- Blank canvas – add your own widgets from scratch
- Starter dashboard – populated with example widgets
- Import from gallery – import dashboards shared by others

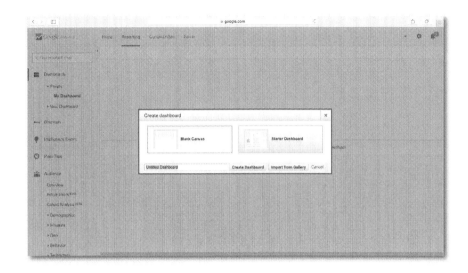

To get started with useful dashboards quickly, find some readymade ones using the Import from Gallery option.

In the example below, I imported Occam's Razor Awesomeness from the shared gallery, which added the VP, Digital dashboard to my dashboards list.

From any dashboard (either a new or existing) you can click on the Add Widget button to add a new element to the display.

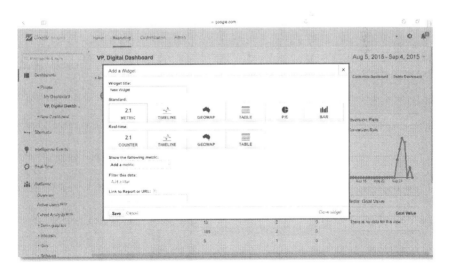

For example, create a timeline widget showing clicks versus bounce rate, using the settings from the screenshot below.

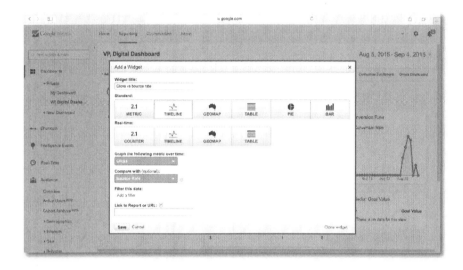

This adds a new widget to the dashboard. You can move and position the widgets as you like using drag and drop.

Chapter summary

This chapter explained how you can measure goal and campaign results, and create your own custom dashboards. The next chapter will continue with advanced web metrics using Google Analytics.

Web analytics 3 - Advanced concepts

In this chapter, we will go one step further and see what Google Analytics can do in terms of integration with other online and offline data sources, and look into some other advanced capabilities.

Search engine effectiveness

The Google Search Console (previously called Google Webmaster Tools, found at **https://www.google.com/webmasters/** tools) provides various services to website owners, including:

- Submit a sitemap to help Google index your website better
- Check for broken links
- See what search keywords listed your web pages in SERPs

You can link your Google Analytics account with your Google Search Console account, thus connecting Google search information with your website analytics data. In practice, this means you can see metrics on how your web pages perform in relation to the Google Search result pages (SERPs) from within Google Analytics.

What search keywords give visibility and visitors?

In the Queries report of Google Analytics [Acquisition > Search Engine Optimization > Queries], you can see what Google search keywords have resulted in your web pages being listed in the search result list.

The main graph shows the number of times pages from your website are shown in Google search results pages each day. Below the graph, you can see what phrases result in your website pages being listed in the Google search results pages, along with information on:

- How many times a page on your website was visible in Google search results for that search keyword phrase
- How many clicks they got
- The average page rank for your pages listed for each search phrase
- The click-through rate

In short, this report is the grand dashboard for understanding how well your web pages are visible to Google search users.

By selecting the +/- comparison graph display option (to the right of the search field), you can easily visualize how many clicks a specific web page get from search engine result pages compared to the average on your website. Since the table is sorted by the number of impressions, you can easily weed out the pages that are displayed in search result pages often, but get a lower-than-average number of clicks.

Pages that are displayed in search engine results pages often but don't get many clicks have an ineffective title or page description, causing search users to click on something else instead. Look into it and correct the problem.

If your pages end up in the Google search results pages rarely, and with low-ranking positions, almost no visitors will find you. Make sure to write a lot of new content (blog articles are perfect here), each targeting the keywords the page should be optimized for. The screenshot above, for example, show little search traffic, as the screenshot was taken from a brand new website with few visitors at this early point.

If the desired keywords have tough competition, try longer-tailed keywords for better success. With some delay, this will help improve the situation. The other option is to pay for traffic using paid advertisement campaigns.

What web pages perform best?

In the Landing Pages report [Acquisition > Search Engine Optimization > Landing pages], you can see what pages on your website get most of the visibility and activity from Google searches.

You can see the number of times each page has been displayed in the Google search results pages, the number of clicks driving organic traffic to the web page, the average rank in the Google search results pages, and the average click-through rate (CTR).

Pages with many impressions in the Google search results pages, but with a low click-through rate, do not have a heading or description that attracts people to jump to your web page. Look into this and try to improve the click-through rate, as it is an excellent opportunity to get more visitors for free.

Event tracking

By instrumenting your web pages with some additional HTML elements (not the normal Google Analytics tracking code), you can use Google Analytics to track all sorts of user events in great detail, not just pageviews. Things that can be tracked include:

- Clicks on buttons, hyperlinks, images, banner ads, etc.
- File downloads
- Form engagement
- Page consumption
- Emails
- Phone calls
- Mobile app usage

Events are grouped in categories of your choice, such as Button Clicks, PDF Downloads, Form Field Completions, and more. The exact details on how to add the event tracking code to your web pages are too technical for this book, but search for "Google Analytics event tracking" if you want to know how. It requires a bit of HTML coding to do properly.

With the event tracking code added, you can see the event statistics in the Event Overview report [Behavior > Events > Overview].

Tracking clicks

One of the most popular types of events to track is mouse-clicks. For example, this can be a click on:

- Hypertext links
- Buttons
- Images (for example banner ads)
- PDF or document download links
- Play, pause or stop control buttons of videos
- Social sharing buttons

Tracking downloads

Assuming you have several files (such as PDF documents) available for download on your website, Google Analytics can help you understand what assets are most popular, and by what group of users. Instrument the download link in exactly the same manner as other clicks are tracked, and Google Analytics can tell you which files are downloaded most often.

184

Tracking forms and form fields

By instrumenting each field in forms with its own event tracking code, you can let Google Analytics show you statistics on what form fields are completed or skipped. This can help you understand how your visitors react to the various form field questions, or on what question they chose to abandon the form.

You can also add some events to the form itself to get more easily consumed data with less detail, such as an event for successful submission and one for a failed submission.

Tracking page content consumption

You can instrument a web page to emit scroll range data to Google Analytics. In effect, scroll-range event tracking will tell you to what extent a web page is read. No scrolling implies the page was visited but not read. If the page has been scrolled halfway, the visitor left without consuming all the content, and a page is probably read to the end if the page has been fully scrolled.

Using this technique, you can list your most popular and unpopular pages in Google Analytics in terms of reader engagement, instead of by pageviews.

Tracking emails

Your website can allow the visitor to contact you by email. This is done either using a mailto link that opens the email client of the visitor, or using a website form that sends an email when the visitor clicks the submit button. In both cases, you can create Google Analytics events that monitor how many emails you get from your website.

To track the results of mass mailings, use the capabilities of email service companies like MailChimp, Campaign Monitor, or Litmus to send emails and track delivery, open, and click-through rates. Some email service providers have advanced analysis capabilities, including real-time views that show on a map where (down to city level) the email is opened, as it happens in real-time.

Tracking phone calls

So far, I have explained what Google Analytics can do for you in terms of measuring website and marketing data. Interestingly, Google Analytics can also gather statistics on other things, such as incoming phone calls to your business. How can this possibly be done? The answer is that the event tracking mechanism discussed above is generic enough that it can be put to unexpected use.

Google Analytics is a powerful platform for visualizing statistics in general, including advanced capabilities for custom dashboards. Therefore, many phone service operators either provide integration with it or provide hooks for sending events, where you can add the Google Analytics event tracking code for various phone call related events.

For example, phone events recorded in Google Analytics can be the number of incoming calls, the number of unanswered calls, the number of calls with duration over 5 minutes, or other data. You can then use the dashboards and other capabilities (goals come to mind here) of Google Analytics to get a detailed picture of how your business performs in terms of phone calls.

Many call service providers offer their own dashboards for phone statistics. Why not use them instead? The main advantage of using Google is that you can easily correlate online marketing activities with phone statistics, and you have all data in one place.

Tracking smartphone or tablet app usage

If you or someone in your company is developing smartphone or tablet apps, you can use Google Analytics here too. Similar to tracking incoming phone calls, the Google Analytics event tracking mechanism can be used to track how users interact with your software product, for example, an iPhone or Android game.

You can track button clicks, menu selections, mobile ad clicks, swipes or other gestures, and video playing. While you can track almost anything, you should probably focus on tracking events relevant to your sales and marketing efforts. The number of times a rifle is fired in a game may be irrelevant from a marketing point of view, but the number of times the user visits the in-app purchase screen to buy additional game levels may be of more use.

Using reports in Google Analytics, you can see how frequently and how recently users come back to your app in a given period, and more.

Tracking other things

As you have probably realized by now, the event tracking mechanism of Google Analytics is generic and can be used for almost anything that can be instrumented with event tracking code.

For example, use it for webshop and shopping cart performance tracking. Do you want to gather statistical data on some offline events relevant to your organization, and correlate it with other website statistics? Create a private web page that only your organization can access, with Google Analytics instrumented buttons that record the offline events when your staff click on the buttons. The possibilities are almost endless.

Intelligence alerts

A major problem with website analytics is the sheer amount of data—how can you find the needle in the haystack? There may be important changes to traffic behavior and new trends that go unnoticed because the information needed to detect it is deep buried in the enormous amounts of data.

In particular, it is interesting to know:

- Are there any considerable changes to the traffic behavior?
- Where should we focus attention?
- Are there any trends we need to detect?
- What important things are we unaware of?

Again, Google Analytics can help. Using the Intelligence Event report [Intelligence Events > Overview] you can spot important changes to visitor behavior that are detected automatically by the built-in intelligence engine.

In effect, using the automatic intelligence alerts in Google Analytics is like having a team of real-time analysts monitoring your website for unexpected changes to visitor behavior. This enables you to detect meaningful signals very quickly.

The intelligence engine performs statistical analysis on previous visitor behavior patterns, and provided a website has sufficient visitor volume, the algorithms can predict what user behaviors are expected in the future. By comparing the actual user patterns to the predicted ones, Google Analytics can detect unexpected changes to traffic behavior, and alert you about them. However, it doesn't work if your traffic volume is too low.

Google Analytics provides both automatic and custom defined alerts. Signals that can be detected are, for example, changes to the visitor, pageview, and bounce rates, conversion rates, geographic or source of traffic, entry and exit pages, referrals, or goal value.

A measure that falls outside the predicted range is reported in the graph, with the option to drill down for additional detail.

A/B testing

One of the best methods to scientifically optimize a website is A/B testing, where two versions of a page are tested against each other using a random sample of users. The aim is to use the winning (most popular) version from then on. Google Analytics provides for A/B testing of web pages, where you can easily compare how two versions of a page perform.

For example, you can test what performs best between a top or left menu, a blue or red color scheme, or what heading or image triggers more form submissions. You can setup A/B testing in Google Analytics using the Behavior Experiment report [Behavior > Experiment].

Click the Create Experiment button and give it a name. Define two or more page variations (URLs) to compare, and add the A/B testing tracking code provided by Google Analytics to the page variations.

Once A/B testing experiments are defined, you can track their progress using the Behavior Experiment report.

It takes a while before the results are available. Select the A/B testing experiment you want to analyze using the Behavior Experiments report [Behavior > Experiments].

For example, the A/B testing experiment below tests the relative performance of a blue and red version of a newsletter registration form.

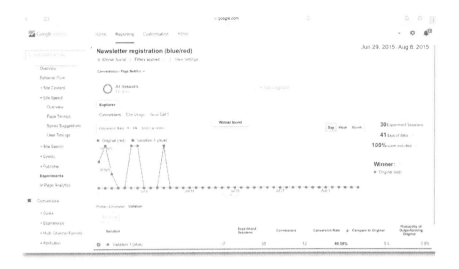

As can be seen in the screenshot above, the red version of the newsletter registration form (the blue line in the graph) has not triggered a single goal conversion. The blue version (the orange line in the graph) has generated some and become the winner.

Website speed

You may want to study your website speed performance. A slow website does not give your users a great experience. It also punishes your ranking in the Google search results pages.

The speed performance of your website can be analyzed using the Site Speed report [Behavior > Site Speed > Overview]. Unfortunately, Google defaults to analyzing only a small fraction of the traffic, and it may take considerable time before you get any useful data unless you have a lot of traffic to your website.

The main graph shows the average page load time while the small sparklines show more detailed information on various aspects of the website speed.

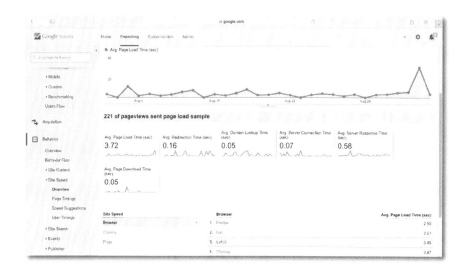

Using the Page Timing report [Behavior > Site Speed > Page Timing], you can see the average timing for each page, with information on how it compares to the average.

In the Speed Suggestions report [Behavior > Site Speed > Speed Suggestions], Google has analyzed all your web pages and provides suggestions on how you can improve the performance for each of them. Click the link in the PageSpeed Suggestions column to get a recommendation of what you can do for each particular page.

Chapter summary

This chapter has shown how Google Analytics can be used for advanced analytics. The next chapter will outline some other Internet tools that can be helpful in making your marketing campaigns more effective.

Other Internet marketing tools

In addition to the ones we discussed earlier, Internet marketers may need to use other tools occasionally. This chapter describes some that you may find useful.

Surveys and questionnaires

Sometimes it is useful to gather customer feedback or to make market surveys. Internet forms are helpful for this. There are many free and paid Internet survey services available, and the most well-known is SurveyMonkey.

With SurveyMonkey and other similar solutions, you can define a set of questions you want to ask. In addition to the question label, you can specify the answer type, such as a checkbox, radio buttons, or a drop-down list of predefined values for each question. You can also define your own company logotype on the top of the survey page (which is usually hosted on their web servers, not yours).

More advanced features include branch logic, where answers to previous questions affect what questions will be asked later. A/B testing can be supported, where you can see how a different questionnaire setup affects the outcome.

These tools are easy to use, and a simple customer feedback survey can be setup in minutes. You are usually given good statistics and results reports as well.

An Internet survey obviously has no value unless you get people to take part in it. It must be promoted, typically using emails to existing leads or customers, or by advertising on the website or in the blog.

Most survey solution providers provide good report visualization tools, enabling you to analyze the answers.

Virtual meetings and seminars

If you work in a geographically spread market, it may be expensive or even impossible to meet up with prospective customers, existing customers, suppliers, resellers, or other partners. The Internet has proven very useful in this scenario too, as it is now very cheap and easy to set up phone calls, meetings, and seminars remotely.

The most well-known solution for free international calls over the Internet is Skype. Microsoft now owns the service, but Skype apps are available for all major platforms, including Windows, Mac OS X, iOS, and Android. In addition to calling for free anywhere in the world, Skype also allows you to include more people in the call, effectively providing a telephone conference system at no cost. In addition to voice calls, Skype supports video calls too.

Skype also allows you to share your screen, such that the other people in the call will see your PowerPoint presentation or other types of demonstrations. In my experience, Skype is fantastic for free international phone calls but is a little weak on screen-sharing for serious Internet meetings.

An unexpected strength of Skype is its file transfer capability. I can't remember how many times I have tried to email large files (in particular videos), only to have the email bounce back undelivered due to oversized file attachments. Skype can easily transfer a huge file between two people, quickly rescuing the situation.

However, Skype is still a bit weak for serious Internet meetings with many attendees and screen sharing. There are more professional web meeting services available, including WebEx from Cisco and GotoMeeting from Citrix.

Using this type of tool, you can run virtual meetings over the Internet with the option for screen sharing and even remote control of other computers in the meeting. This is perfect if you do remote technical support of computer software. You may sit in your London office and remote control a customer's PC in Hong Kong to troubleshoot a problem.

Dedicated web meeting systems can often record the session for later viewing. If you have a webcam, you can share a video stream of yourself or something else. Both WebEx and GotoMeeting allow meeting attendees to dial-in for free using voice over IP (VoIP, phone calls over the internet). Use a headset or the mic and speakers in your computer, or using local landline dial-in numbers in different countries.

Interactive self-running presentations and demos

There are now solutions for interactive, self-running demos, most notably DemoChimp. With DemoChimp, you can distribute self-running interactive videos, such as product demos or sales presentations.

These videos provide real-time personalization, where each viewer first answers a set of questions on what interests him or her most. Depending on the answers, the movie will show a different set of "chapters", such that each viewer gets to see a personalized movie that focuses on what is important to them.

If you sell software development tools, for example, the development manager, project manager, software developer, and software tester may not be equally interested in all parts of your product demo. With DemoChimp, they can all get to see a different self-running demo or presentation based on how they answered the initial questions.

This means you can distribute just one video, which changes content depending on what each viewer answers in the embedded questionnaire before they watch it.

Chapter summary

This chapter outlined some additional tools used in Internet marketing, including Internet surveys, web meetings, and interactive media. The next chapter looks at how the Internet marketing landscape might evolve in the coming years.

The future of Internet marketing

Predicting the future is never an exact science, but it doesn't take a rocket scientist to predict some of what lies ahead. In this chapter, I make some guesses.

Predictive marketing automation systems

Advanced marketing automation systems are still cutting-edge and have so far not been used by most small and medium sized companies. It can be assumed they will become mainstream and more companies will start to use them.

The capabilities of these systems will improve over time, and I foresee marketing automation systems integrating with many more types of systems in the future, deepening the integration of data from various sources.

Additionally, I think these systems will become smarter with more predictive analysis and predictive intelligence. Systems will be able to learn as more data becomes available and adjust their behavior automatically. This is similar to how Netflix learns from your behavior and recommends better movies as it gets more data on your preferences.

Smart, adaptive content

Marketing content will increasingly become more intelligent. For example, movies or slideshows will adapt automatically based on visitor behavior or other types of lead profiling information.

In addition to movies or slideshows, other kinds of marketing content will probably become smart too, and I think we will soon see a lot more interactive or adaptive advertisements.

Big data

Big data is a relatively new, and very interesting, concept. It is about processing massive amounts of information recorded for one purpose, to find valuable data patterns that can be used for other, unrelated, purposes.

For example, Google may detect a certain disease is about to break out in Seattle, based on the number of people from that area that start to search for related topics. My bet is that Google will know about it long before the health authorities because people will look for information on the Internet days before they visit the hospital. There are many other types of big data scenarios too, of course, both using in-house or purchased data from external suppliers.

Marketers may be able to tap into data gathered from big data analysis, and adjust marketing messages accordingly, perhaps even in real-time.

The Internet of Things (IoT)

The Internet of Things (IoT) is the next big hype. IoT is about connecting everyday products to the Internet. This can include consumer products, household appliances, industrial sensors, transportation infrastructure, or computer systems in vehicles.

McKinsey predicts a whopping 1 trillion devices will be Internet-connected by 2025. This enables behavior or usage patterns from all sorts of products to be recorded, and at least some of this data will be made available to Internet marketers. Your bathroom scale may trigger advertisements for healthy food or health club memberships, for example.

This is not a joke. I recently bought a bathroom scale that connects to the Internet and uploads information on my weight to a website. I can log in to get all sorts of nice graphs plotting my weight history. I am very happy with it, and while the data is not used for marketing purposes (I think!), it is an example of what probably lies ahead.

Web analytics on everything

Web analytics will be deployed to an even greater level, and website users will be tracked across mediums like websites, mobile apps, social media, or content publishing sites.

Usage data from billions of IoT devices will almost for sure be integrated and tracked using web analytics tools too. This is already possible to do for smartphone and tablet apps. Google likely has big aspirations for the IoT market, so you can expect Google Analytics to integrate IoT usage information in the future too.

Final thoughts

Internet marketers live in exciting times. There are so many possibilities, and small companies can excel and beat larger competitors if they use smart marketing and analytics intelligently.

In many ways, the future is already here and the capabilities are almost endless. There are some privacy and security concerns as more and more personal data is gathered and cross-referenced, and I am sure the industry and legislation will start to address these issues.

Make the best use of all the tools and techniques at your disposal, in a responsible manner, and improve your business success!

I had so much fun writing this book, and I hope you found it useful. Early on in the project, I decided to pursue self-publishing, meaning the book has no publishing house helping to promote it. For self-published authors, getting many book reviews is critical to building the success needed to write more books. If you want to support me or this book, please give an honest review and star rating on Amazon. I would be most grateful and it will help me enormously.

If you have any feedback, good or bad, that you would like to share with me personally, you can find my contact information after the appendices.

APPENDIX 1: Internet networking basics

This book is about marketing, not technology, but some engineering knowledge might be needed. Please bear with me as we cover the basics about the underlying technologies that make online marketing a possibility.

IP addresses

The Internet is all about computers talking to each other. How does one computer know how to communicate with another computer somewhere else on the Internet? It is quite straightforward. On the Internet, every computer has an identification number, called the IP address. By knowing the IP address of a computer, you also know how to find it on the Internet.

Historically (using IPv4), the IP addresses have been stored in a dot-separated 32-bit number (don't worry if this is all mumbo jumbo to you). For example, a computer might have the address 172.16.254.1 on the Internet. The problem for the IT industry is that the world is quickly running out of available IP-addresses, as there are now billions of computers. More IP addresses do not fit in the standardized 32-bit number range used in IPv4.

To make matters worse, the world is about to enter the era of Internet of Things (IoT) where not only computers but also other types of devices are Internet connected. This can be cars, smart watches, bathroom scales, coffee machines, industrial sensors, TV-sets, light bulbs, and much more. This only adds to the problem of IPv4 running out of available addresses.

To solve the problem of IP address shortage, the Internet industry is now moving from the old IPv4 address system to the new IPv6 address system. IPv6 uses 128-bits for storage and thus can support a much larger number of addresses. An IPv6 computer address may look like this: 2001:db8:0:1234:0:567:8:1.

You can safely ignore the details of IPv4 or IPv6, just keep in mind that every computer or device on the Internet has a unique identification number called an IP address. By knowing the IP address, you can find it and communicate with it.

Domain names and subdomains

While IP addresses are enough from a technical point of view, they are impractical to use for human beings. For example, would you like to browse the CNN website by entering their IP address 185.31.17.73 in the web browser address field? Do you remember the IP address of the Spotify streaming music service? I think not.

To solve this problem, an Internet standard called the Domain Name System (DNS) is used. This is a simple table that lines names to IP addresses. In the DNS databases, CNN have registered their domain name cnn.com to be equal to the IP address of their web server, which at the time of writing was 185.31.17.73.

Typing 185.31.17.73 or www.cnn.com in the address field of your web browser gives the same result; they are just a numeric and textual version of the same thing. In both cases, the web browser shows you the CNN website.

If the IP address is the formal street address of a house, the domain name is a short easy-to-remember label for it, like the San Francisco Airport or Apple headquarters. Examples of domain names are cnn.com, netfix.com, apple.com, ibm.com, etc.

But if a domain name can only be connected to one IP address (and hence one computer), how can large corporations spread their public IT services over several server computers while still keeping them under the same hat of their corporate .com domain name? Surely companies like Apple or IBM have more than one server?

There are various technologies to sort this out at different levels of complexity, but for the purpose of online marketing of small businesses, only one is relevant: subdomains. This book teaches you to use a website and a blog, and for various reasons, it may well be that they are hosted on different server computers. But you still want to use your company domain name (such as mycompany.com) for both to keep your marketing message together, and for other reasons, like search engine optimization.

To enable several servers to use the same domain name, the DNS standard allows subdomains, where different computers (hence using different IP addresses) can connect themselves to various parts of your mycompany.com domain name. This is done by hooking a unique prefix in front of the domain name.

For example, you may connect your website using www.mycompany.com to a web server on IP address 183.45.3.122 while you connect your blog using blog.mycompany.com to a blogging server on IP address 122.77.54.23.

In effect, you have created subdomains under your mycompany.com domain, each pointing to different servers:

	IP address	Subdomain
Website webserver	183.45.3.122	www.mycompany.com
Blog webserver	122.77.54.23	blog.mycomany.com

By entering www.mycompany.com or blog.mycompany.com in your web browser, you end up in different websites, run by various web servers, even though they both use the same domain name to keep your marketing message together.

Ports

You now know how the IP address identifies a computer on the Internet, and that a domain name (or a subdomain) is a more convenient text label pointing to the same thing.

To make matters a little bit more complicated, in reality computers do not talk to other computers on the Internet after all. Instead, software programs on a computer talk to other software programs on another computer. If a computer has more than one program that wants to talk to the Internet (the web browser, the email client, and Skype, for example), how do programs find the right program to talk to another computer?

This is done by assigning a number called an IP port to the programs running in a computer. To communicate with a specific software program on another computer, you really need to know both the IP address and the IP port. The IP address brings you to the right computer, and the IP port brings you to the right program running in it.

If the IP address is the address of the building, the IP port is the apartment number inside it. The port number is written after the IP address or domain name with a separating colon, for example 192.45.3.55:20 or www.mycompany.com:20.

Port numbers are standardized for certain software services like web surfing. Unless you explicitly use a different port number in the address bar of your web browser, it will default to the standardized port number for web browsing (port 80), and therefore the web browser and webserver know how to communicate, even if you do not add the port number to the address bar. They both default to use port 80 for web browsing communications.

Uniform resource locators (URLs)

A URL is a reference to a file. It specifies the location of the file on the network, and the method to retrieve it (the Internet protocol to access it). Different Internet protocols are used for different purposes, such as HTTP (Hypertext transfer protocol) for web browsing or FTP (file transfer protocol) for file copying.

Web browsers usually display the URL of a web page in an address bar above the page itself. A URL is formatted like http://www.example.com/index.html. This includes the protocol type (HTTP), the domain name, (www.example.com), and the particular web page file (index.html).

If it makes things easier, you can see the URL as the location and name of a file on the Internet.

APPENDIX 2: Website basics

With the networking details out of the way, I want to provide a brief overview of some other Internet technologies more related to website design and implementation. This is not a book on website development, but a minimum understanding is needed if you want to do Internet marketing at any practical level.

Websites

Your website is at the heart of any Internet marketing strategy. A website is a collection of web pages, each of which is implemented as an HTML file that contains the web page contents (text and hypertext links) as well as references to other resources like images or movies. The top (main or front) web page is called the home page.

A small website contains just one or a few web pages, while a large website can contain thousands. Websites typically have menus to aid navigation across the different pages.

A hot topic with website design in the last couple of years is responsiveness, and the growing need to have a responsive website. In this context, it has nothing to do with waiting times after you click with the mouse somewhere. Instead, it refers to the capability of a website to auto-adjust its layout to make it fit better for mobile devices with small screens.

A traditional website looks the same on a PC and a smartphone (and so you need to zoom and pan all the time if you use a small screen). A responsive website automatically rearranges blocks of information so that they are stacked after each other, providing a narrower and taller website if visited from a mobile device with a small screen.

No book on websites can avoid mentioning the three cornerstones of a website: HTML, CSS, and JavaScript. Each will be outlined briefly below. Unless you design a website on your own, you do not need to understand any details. But you will hear about HTML, CSS, and JavaScript all the time, so it is useful to have at least a rough idea of what they are. I have added a section on cookies too, as they are used a lot by websites, marketing automation systems, and web analytics tools.

HTML

Each web page on a website is implemented as an HTML file. HTML is a styling and content language. HTML files contain the human readable information on a web page, as well as formatting and styling code such fonts or colors, images, hypertext links, or tables.

In the early days, webmasters had to add the HTML tags manually using a text editor, but nowadays HTML pages are typically edited using a WYSIWYG (what you see is what you get) editor. Writing a web page today should give more or less the same experience as editing a text in a word processor like Microsoft Word.

A problem with HTML is that the graphical layout, formatting, and human readable information are mixed, and there is no support for consistent formatting or styling across a web page or site. CSS was introduced to resolve this problem.

CSS

Cascading style sheets (CSS) is a style and layout description language. It is an attempt to remove (most of) the layout and formatting information from the human readable content of the HTML files into a separate description file, thus creating a clear separation of the graphical design from the human readable information.

Since many HTML files can share (more technically, refer to) the same CSS file, it is easy to create a consistent graphical profile. If you change the graphical profile once (in the CSS file), it automatically applies to all HTML pages across the full website.

JavaScript

JavaScript is a programming language used to add dynamic behavior to web pages. Small or large snippets of JavaScript code are injected into the HTML code to enable dynamic behavior such as tooltips, expanding or folding menus, slideshows, animations, querying databases for dynamic content, and more.

The JavaScript code embedded into HTML pages is executed by the web browser. There are many JavaScript code examples available on the Internet that can be reused, as well as libraries of JavaScript functionalities that can be used to easily add more extensive functionalities.

HTML5

HTML5 is the latest version of the HTML standard, and the name HTML5 is often used when referring to the latest HTML, CSS, and JavaScript technologies used together as well.

In particular, HTML5 adds many capabilities in terms of multimedia (sound and video), as well as graphics and complex web applications (for example, support for drag and drop) compared to older versions.

Cookies

You have probably heard of cookies before. A cookie is a small piece of information a website can send to the web browser of a website visitor. The web browser will store the cookie on the user's computer, and each time the user comes back to the same website, the browser sends the cookie back to the website to notify it about previous activity.

The use of cookies has been debated due to privacy concerns, and many countries make websites notify users of their cookie use by law. Cookies themselves are not dangerous, and they do no harm to the computer, but they do allow a website to track user activity.

Cookies are used for key functionalities on the web. For example, remembering if a user is logged in or not to a website, remembering user configuration settings of a website, and tracking user behavior for later analysis.

Webservers

A web server is technically a software service (i.e., a program) that runs on a computer, but it can also denote the physical computer in which the software is running. A web server (the software) accepts download requests from web browsers and returns the various web pages that are to be displayed in your web browser when you visit a website.

A web server delivers the web pages (HTML files) to your web browser when you visit a web site (technically, it also delivers other files, like CSS files and images). Website developers have to use relatively low-level webserver software like Apache when building and maintaining a website in this traditional way.

Creating a web page requires editing an HTML file with human readable text and HTML metadata tags using an editor. Once the HTML file is finally completed, the HTML file must be copied (published) to a public location on the web server, making the new web page available using a web browser from anywhere in the world.

This is cumbersome for two reasons. First, the editing of the web page is done on a low abstraction level, and secondly, an IT server administrator must give you access rights to upload the new HTML file to it.

Nowadays, it is unusual for normal websites to be built in this traditional way, using just a webserver. The industry needed something much easier to use, and the salvation came in the form of Content Management Systems (CMS).

Content management systems

A content management system includes a web server, but expands upon it and adds a WYSIWYG (what you see is what you get) web page editor. It also provides a web-based admin interface, allowing you to add or edit pages, change the menu structure, and more without any programming knowledge.

Technically, a CMS is a web server that stores the web pages in a database rather than using HTML files. The CMS provides a web-based interface to create and edit the pages stored in the database. By using a database driven CMS, almost anyone can maintain a website by adding or changing web pages, menu options, and more, as needed.

There are many CMS systems available on the market, and the two most popular are WordPress and Joomla. Both are open-source software that can be downloaded for free from the Internet, for installation in your own server computers. However, a better approach for small businesses is to rent a readymade WordPress or Joomla hosting solution. That way you do not need to worry about installing server hardware and software, backups, security solutions like intrusion detection systems, or firewalls.

WordPress is an easy-to-use CMS that started as a blogging platform. By now it is the most popular CMS for small websites.

Joomla has traditionally been more powerful, and a bit more difficult to learn as a consequence. Joomla is the most popular CMS after WordPress.

So which one to use? Both are free of charge, and both can be installed on your own server or rented as a hosted service at low cost. Both have thousands of plugins that can be installed to extend their functionalities in any direction, and both have thousands of themes that can be installed to change the look and feel of your website.

It typically comes down to preference, but one could generalize and say that WordPress is better for novice users creating a smaller website, while Joomla is better suited for larger websites requiring somewhat stronger capabilities.

The good news is, both have excellent resources on the Internet, like user support forums, and there are many books explaining how to use them both.

Feedback and contacting the author

I hope you have found this book useful, and while I have made every effort to provide as valuable and error-free knowledge as possible, no product is perfect and it can always be improved.

If you have any feedback, good or bad, I would appreciate hearing from you. With reader feedback, I can improve future versions of this book for the benefit of other readers. I can be contacted using the email address **feedback@unemyr.com**.

I look forward to hearing from you!

You may also want to visit my website and blog at **www.unemyr.com**. My Facebook profile is "Magnus Unemyr the Author", and you can sign up for my newsletter here:

http://www.unemyr.com/sign-up-for-newsletter/

Thank you for reading.

Acknowledgements

I would like to thank my wonderful partner Anita for being understanding during all the late nights and weekends it took to write this book. I also want to thank her for the feedback she gave me, based on her experience as a journalist.

Additionally, I want to thank my parents and brother for being supportive and teaching me the value and good results of consistent and hard work.

And finally, I would like to thank Eric for the great editing services, Henrik for the cover art design, and Mattias, Nils and Erik for the reviews of my drafts. You all know who you are.

Without you this book would not have been possible.

Thank you!

Printed in Great Britain
by Amazon